DISCOVERING
PATCHWORK

By Rosamond Richardson
and Erica Griffiths

Photographed by Ed Buziak
Illustrated by Diana Groves

BRITISH BROADCASTING CORPORATION

Detail of a cover made of silks in a pattern called
Baby Blocks or sometimes Tumbling Blocks. It was
made in England around 1870 and is a good example
of Victorian patchwork (see p. 47).

This book accompanies the BBC Television series
'Discovering Patchwork' first broadcast on BBC-2
in January 1978
Produced by Erica Griffiths and Peter Riding
Published to accompany a series of programmes
prepared in consultation with
the BBC Continuing Education Advisory Council

Published by the British Broadcasting Corporation
35 Marylebone High Street, London W1M 4AA
ISBN 0 563 16212 0 First published 1977
reprinted 1978 (three times), 1979, 1981
© Rosamond Richardson and
the British Broadcasting Corporation 1977.
Printed in England by
Alan Pooley Printing Ltd, Tonbridge, Kent.
This book is set in 10 on 12pt Plantin Monophoto

Front cover: A quilt made in Lancaster County,
Pennsylvania, USA between 1880 and 1890. The design
is called Trip Around the World. (For instructions
on how to make this quilt, see p. 57.)

CONTENTS

The measurements given in this book are in metric
with the imperial sizes in brackets. These are *not*
exact equivalents so you must either work
completely in metric or completely in imperial
when following the instructions for any one article.

A BRIEF HISTORY

Patchwork is the art of cutting scraps of fabric into geometric shapes and sewing them together to make up a mosaic surface. Perhaps the best known form of patchwork is the patchwork quilt, but in fact this is a combination of two separate crafts. A quilt may or may not be patched, and patchwork may or may not be quilted. This book deals only with the craft of patchwork, which is also known as pieced work, and you will need to consult other books for quilting techniques (see book list p. 64).

Fabrics are known to have existed in Neolithic times (6000 B.C.) in Anatolia but because they are a perishable product, comparatively little remains from early days. The earliest known example of *patchwork* was found in the Cave of the Thousand Buddhas in India and dates from between the 6th and 9th Centuries A.D.

The Crusaders of the 11th and 12th Centuries are believed to have brought the art of patchwork back to England from the Middle East, but no examples of that period remain, although there are references to patchwork in early literature. The first surviving example of English patchwork is the Levens Hall coverlet at Kendal, made in 1708 from Indian calicoes (see below).

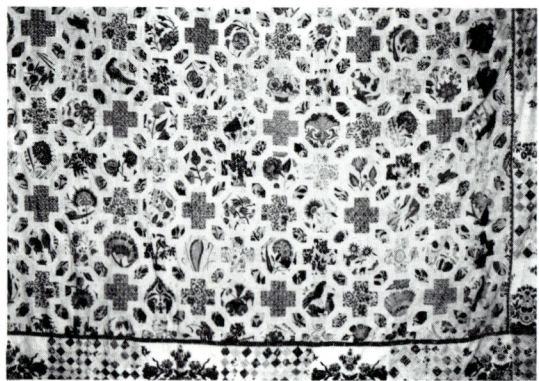

Patchwork is a salvage art, and since its original function was to provide warmth economically, its development has been closely associated with climate. The Great Freeze of the 14th Century altered ways of clothing, and during winter after desperate winter, extra bedcoverings were needed for warmth and comfort. At first, scraps saved from old clothes and furnishings were used to piece the coverlets together, but when materials began to be imported from the East in the 17th and 18th Centuries, their variety changed the whole concept of patchwork into one of creative design. After about 1650, Indian cottons were in great demand in England. The cloth was printed with fine designs and good dyes – calico from Calicut on the south west coast of India, and chintz, a name derived from the Hindi word 'chint' meaning variegated. Soon printers in the West began to imitate the designs and by the middle of the 18th Century thousands of bolts of cotton were being woven around Manchester and sent down for bleaching in the fields near London before printing.

In the Low Countries and Britain, patchwork thrived as a home craft and cottagers made coverlets not only for themselves but also for the nobility. In time, the leisured classes developed the piecing together of scraps of material into a social grace, and the patchwork cover, a highly prized possession, often became a family heirloom. Jane Austen, with her mother and her sister Cassandra, made a coverlet in 1811 of printed cottons in a pattern of diamonds. George Eliot expressed a dismal view of the craft, through Maggie Tulliver in the 'Mill on the Floss': 'It's foolish work', said Maggie with a toss of her mane, 'tearing things to pieces to sew 'em together again'. But it was in the New World, in the two centuries after the Pilgrim Fathers set sail in 1620, that the full potential of these geometric shapes was to be explored with an astonishing development of creative talent.

The migrants who set sail from Britain and

the Low Countries for an unknown continent took with them familiar possessions and native ideas, but they were to face the unremittingly bleak prospect of pioneer life for many generations. This challenge, tempered by thrift which was demanded not only by the rigours of the time but also by a puritanical religious outlook, found expression for the women in patchwork and quilting. The loneliness of their way of life drew them together over the common pursuit of needlework, and soon a lively cultural phenomenon developed which was as much a social occasion as a chance to employ their creative skills. The settlers lived close to nature which was often cruel and unpredictable; perhaps the women found comfort in the use of geometric shapes in their needlework, for although the variety of combinations is enormous, their regularity is a contrast to the chaotic difficulties of settling in an unknown land. At first, they used imported fabrics because the American cotton crop was not established until the 1720s. These were expensive and used with great care, since pre-Revolutionary British rule forbade weaving in the colonies. It was during the long winter months that the women sewed their patchwork patterns, usually in blocks of about a foot square. The block pattern is characteristic of American patchwork: each design is sewn into a square which is easy to handle, then all the blocks are sewn together in various ways to build up a coverlet. In the spring, everyone would come together for feasting and some co-operative effort – the men, perhaps, would put up a barn and the women would gather for what they called their 'quilting bee'. They would sit around a quilting frame to quilt the patchwork done during the winter. Girls were taught to sew as young as three years old, and it became a tradition for a young woman to have made twelve coverlets for her 'bottom drawer' – the thirteenth was the bridal quilt. Men on their twenty-first birthday were presented with the Freedom Quilt, made for them by mothers,

sisters and aspiring girl friends, to be put away for the bride-to-be. One charming tradition was to include a deliberate mistake in the design of a block, which was done to show that man is fallible and only God is perfect.

Patchwork patterns developed names as they travelled across America. Some were inspired by nature, such as Bear's Paw, Flock of Geese and Swallow; some by politics, as Queen Charlotte's Crown and Lincoln's Platform; some by the Indians, as Indian Hatchet and Indian Trail; some by the Bible, as Jacob's Ladder and King David's Crown; and some by everyday life, such as Windmill and Puss in the Corner. The same patterns are called by different names in varying parts of America. The golden age of patchwork, both in this country and in America, spanned the hundred years between 1775 and 1875. The middle classes had increasingly more leisure to pursue various 'genteel' occupations and patchwork ceased to be solely a functional craft. By 1900, creative patchwork had burnt itself out, corrupted by the change from an agricultural society into an industrial one. During the First World War, with fewer servants and many women going out to work for the first time, the art nearly died out, but there was a short revival in the 1930s. Today there is another revival with much fine and original work being produced.

Patchwork has as much to offer us today as it had for the pioneers of the craft: the chance to perfect a technical skill; to explore colour and shape in relation to the division of surface with its enormous variety of combinations; to fulfil a creative outlet which may not be satisfied in everyday life; to produce a useful article which is made for the home and is completely individual. The craft can provide a therapeutic release from the pressures of modern life; perhaps it is the ideal prescription for stress.

These squares illustrate how a range of patchwork designs can be developed from just one basic pattern using different combinations of colour and shape. (See p. 9.)

HOW TO START

The key to accurate patchwork is the template. A template is used to form the pattern from which your patches are cut. It is usually made of metal, plastic or stiff card. There are many different shapes – the square, triangle, hexagon and diamond are some of the most popular – and the template must be accurate or your patches won't fit together.

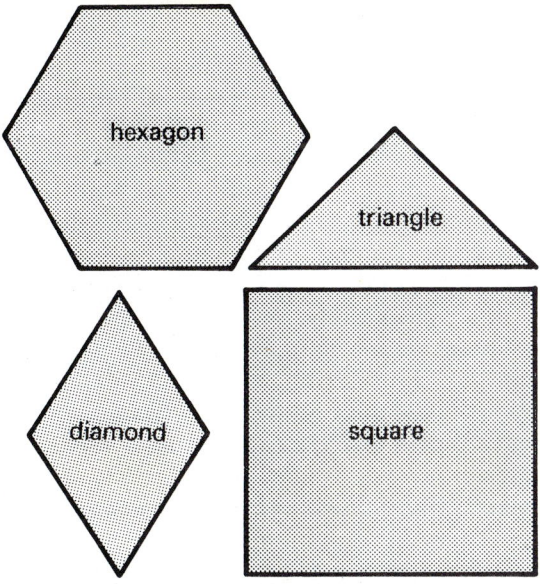

To begin with, you may find it a good idea to buy a few basic templates. Metal or plastic templates in a wide variety of shapes and sizes are available from craft shops. They will keep their accuracy and last a long time.

But if you feel like tackling a bit of simple geometry, you can make your own from stiff card. Instructions for making your own templates are on page 61. Although they won't last as long as bought ones, you can always be sure of having exactly the right sizes available just when you need them.

There are no hard and fast rules about how to make patchwork, and in this book we will be describing the three most commonly used methods. Try them out and see which one suits you best – or experiment with your own personal variations.

These three methods will all be described in more detail in the following chapters, but they are:

1 Hand sewn using paper patterns

This has become the traditional English way of making patchwork. Cut a paper shape from the template (see note on papers on page 8). Pin the paper to your pressed scrap of fabric, with one edge along the straight grain. Cut the fabric with a seam allowance. Turn the material over the edge of the paper and tack all round. Join the patches by placing them right sides together and sewing along the edges to be joined with small, regular oversewing stitches. Don't worry if the stitches show on the right side – this is one of the characteristics of hand sewn patchwork.

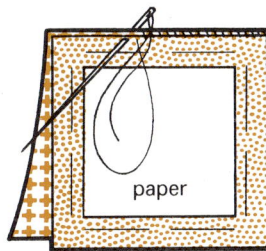

2 Hand sewn without papers

This is the traditional American way of sewing patches together. Put the template on the wrong side of the material and mark around the edge with a pencil. Cut out the patch with a seam allowance. Place the patches right sides together and pin along the matched drawn lines.

Thread a fine needle and make a good knot in the end. Sew up along the pencil line with small, regular running stitches, taking the thread back two stitches for extra security at the end. Press the seam the same way, not open, for strength.

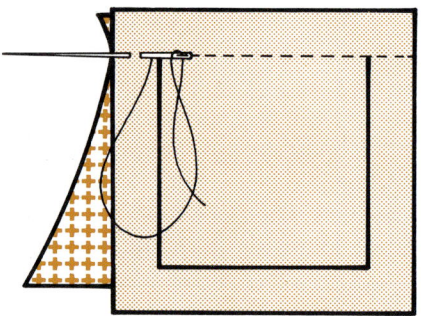

3 Machined patchwork

Cut out the patch in the same way as for (2).
Place the patches right sides together, pin and
machine along the matched drawn lines. Tie
and cut the threads. Press the seam either
open or the same way if you have a number
close together. Machine work gives a harder
seam and a harsher effect, and for small
articles it is not much quicker than sewing by
hand. For larger items, such as a bed cover, it
is obviously a time saver to sew by machine.

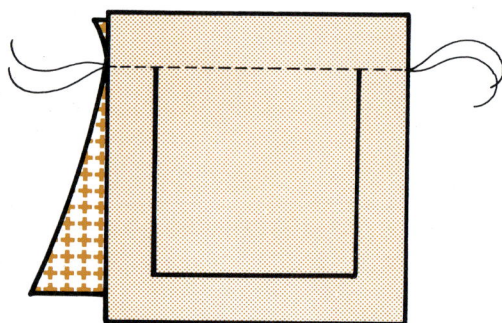

For sewing you will need the following
equipment:

to tack material to paper: tacking thread, size
6 or 7 needles, pins, thimble
to sew patches together: polyester cotton
thread, size 8 or 9 needles, thimble
two pairs of sharp scissors (one for paper, one
for material)
iron and ironing board
sewing machine (optional), tray or newspaper
(useful for carrying your patchwork around on)

Papers

For the paper patterns, you will need thick,
good quality paper such as old envelopes,
letters, cards or uncrumpled brown paper.
Take a sharp pencil or fine ball-point pen and
place the template on the paper. Hold it firmly
down with one hand and draw a line closely
round the sides. Cut along the drawn line with
sharp paper scissors. Check your papers
against the template to make sure the corners
are accurate. If you are drawing a number of
patterns at the same time, make sure you leave
enough space between them to be able to cut
them accurately.

Fabrics

Use fabrics which don't stretch or fray easily
and are of the same weight, preferably with a
fine, even weave. Dress-weight cottons are
ideal for patchwork. Cottons with a high
polyester content are not so successful. They
are too springy to work with easily, the
colours do not blend well with pure cottons
and they press badly. Velvets, silks and fine
wools can be used but are more difficult to
handle. The main thing to avoid is mixing
fabrics of different weights, as a heavy
material next to a fine one may cause the latter
to tear.
Save all your scraps from dress-making,
upholstery and curtain making and keep the
colours separate in plastic bags. You will
almost certainly have to buy new material to
go with your scraps. You will find that your
wardrobe tends to include a limited range of
colours and that for patchwork you will be
short of those colours you never wear. Wash
and press your fabrics before you start your
patchwork. Nothing is more annoying than to
find some of your patches have shrunk after
the first wash.

Colour and design

Colour is an essential part of patchwork and
should be thought out carefully before you
begin. But perhaps even more important than

the colour itself is the *value* of the colour, or the tone of it – that is, how much lighter or darker a piece of material seems to be when placed next to another one. Get into the habit of judging the tone of your materials – try stepping back from them and half closing your eyes. One way of combining materials is to choose colours that are quite close in tone and blend into each other. Another way is to choose a combination of opposites (for example, red and yellow, or black and cream) and more or less stick to it. Jumbling too many colours together can be restless and ugly. But in the end, only *you* know what you really like. When you are selecting your materials, keep in mind the end product and the environment in which it will live, and you will find it will blend and belong.

The possibilities for dividing a surface geometrically are boundless. This is part of the excitement and challenge of patchwork. Look at the examples on page 6. They are all based on one skeleton pattern (see right), but by dividing up the surface in different ways and using different combinations of tones, each square gives a completely different effect.

Try this experiment. The first diagram below is a simple arrangement of nine squares. The next two diagrams show how those nine squares can be changed into completely

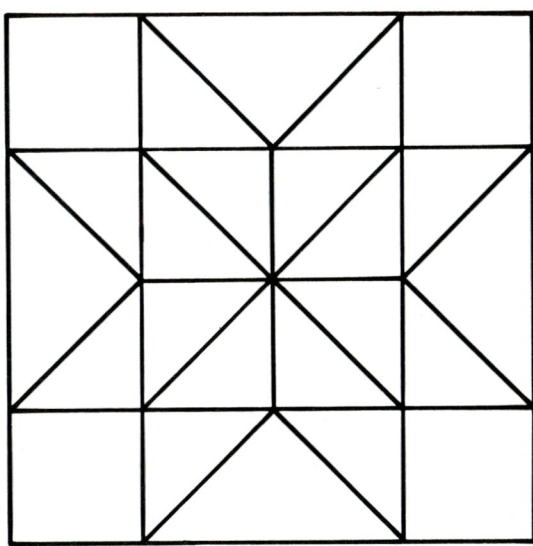

Skeleton pattern for designs on page 6.

different designs by dividing up the surface and using different tones.

Try drawing the block of nine squares three more times, and see how many other variations you can create.

Before you begin to make anything, work out on paper all the possibilities of your design. You don't have to stick rigidly to your final decision, of course. When your patches are ready for sewing up, you may find the material has given the design yet another dimension and you can start juggling the shapes again.

These pincushions, both useful and pretty, are a simple introduction to patchwork. They are rosettes of seven hexagons in plain and printed cotton lawns.

PINCUSHION

This pincushion is made up of seven hexagons on each side and is much more easily and accurately made by hand, using paper patterns, than by machine.

1 To start with, buy or make a hexagon template with sides 2.5 cm (or 1″) in length (see instructions on page 61).

2 Use this template to cut out fourteen paper patterns on good quality thick paper, drawing closely round the template with a sharp pencil and cutting accurately along the lines. When you have cut out the papers, check them for accuracy by holding them against your template.

3 Now choose your materials. You can either make both sides the same or have a contrasting colour scheme on each side. Pick two scraps of plain material for the central patches and six scraps of printed material to go with each plain colour. Try to get a good colour balance by choosing alternating light and dark prints or large and small designs. If some of your materials are striped or checked, or have a directional weave, decide which way you want the lines to go on the finished patch and place your paper pattern accordingly. If you are using floral prints, try to get the flowers in the centre of your patches.

4 When you have chosen your materials, wash and iron them well before you cut out the patches.

5 Pin the paper patterns to the wrong side of the material, leaving about 1 cm (or $\frac{3}{8}$″) around the shape. Cut the fourteen patches with an allowance of 1 cm all the way round (a).

6 Thread a needle with tacking cotton but don't knot the thread. Tack the material to the paper by turning it over the edge of the paper and holding it securely to keep the shape accurate (b). At each corner, fold the material

over the point, making sure it is a tight fit, and put the needle through the fold to keep the material exactly in place (c).

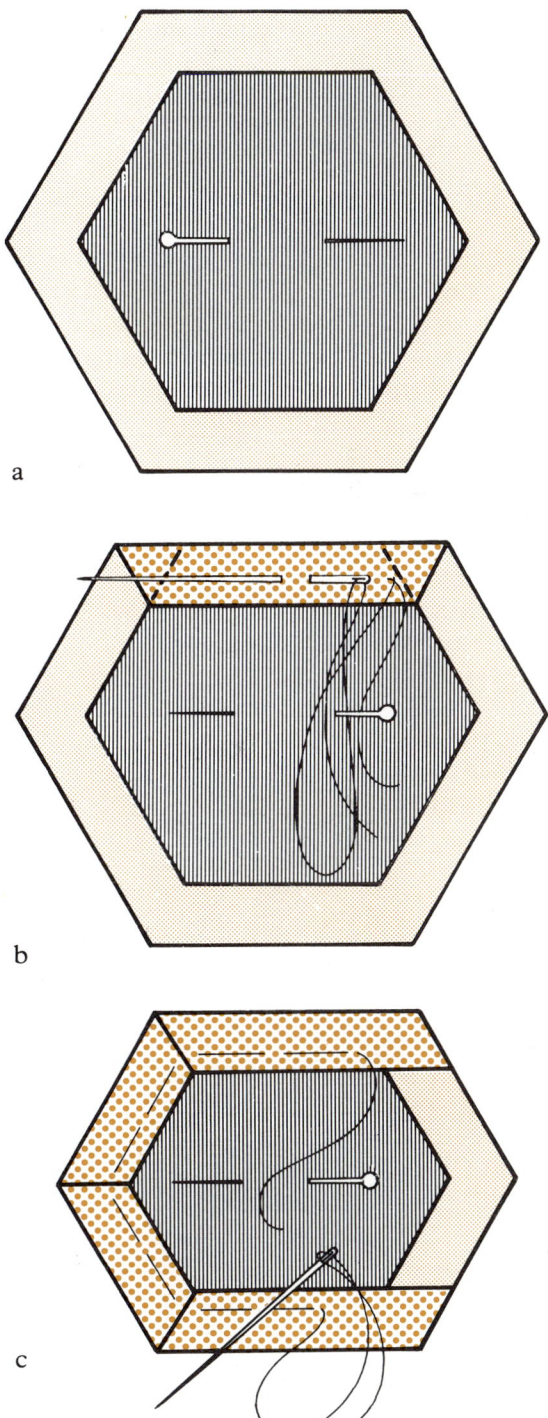

a

b

c

11

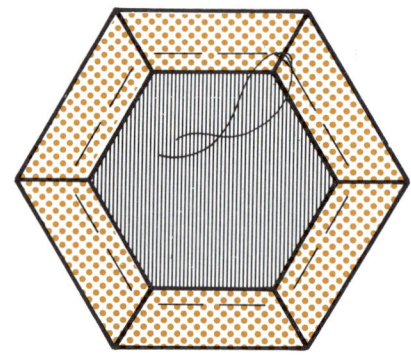

d

Tack all the way round, overlapping the tacking by one stitch and cut the thread without making a backstitch (d). (The absence of knots and backstitches makes it easy to pull out the many tacking threads at the end of the patchwork.)

7 When all the patches are tacked, arrange them on a tray in two rosette shapes. (It is a good idea to keep your patchwork pieces either on a tray or pinned to a piece of newspaper when you're working on it – you can arrange your pieces easily, keep pins, scissors and thread together, and carry it around with you from room to room.) Put the plain patch in the centre, with the prints arranged round it to give a good balance of colour and tone.

8 To sew up the patches, you will need a No. 8 or a No. 9 needle and polyester cotton thread. Make a large knot at the end of your thread. Pick up patches (a) and (b) and place them right sides together exactly on top of each other, making sure the corners match accurately.

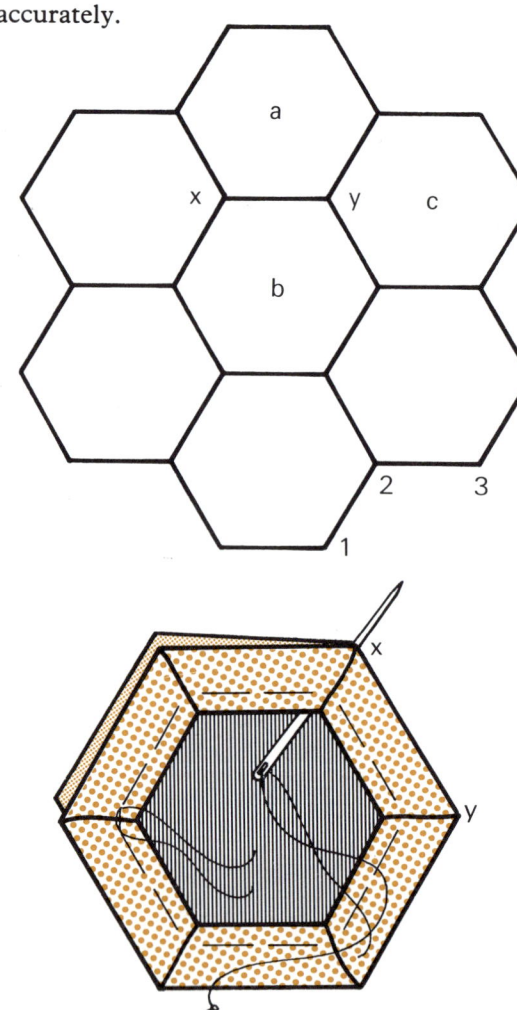

Put the needle in at the corner underneath the material and make a double stitch for strength at the corner. Sew with small, even, firm oversewing stitches to join the two edges from (x) to (y), and make a double stitch again at the corner (y). Try not to sew through the paper patterns as these can be used again. Open the two shapes out, take the next patch (c) and place right sides together with (a) and stitch up in the same way, always making a double stitch at the corners. Then stitch (c) to (b). Continue until one side of the pincushion is completed. The double stitches are important to help the patchwork take the strain of the stuffing. Make the reverse side in exactly the same way.

9 When both sides are finished, place them right sides together with the papers still in place, matching the corners exactly. Sew round the outside edge with small oversewing stitches from point 1 to point 3, leaving the edge 1-2-3 open in a V-shape.

10 Pull out the tacking threads and lift out the papers. If they are undamaged and still accurate, they can be used again. Turn the pincushion inside out so that the wrong sides are together, and poke out the corners with a pair of small scissors.

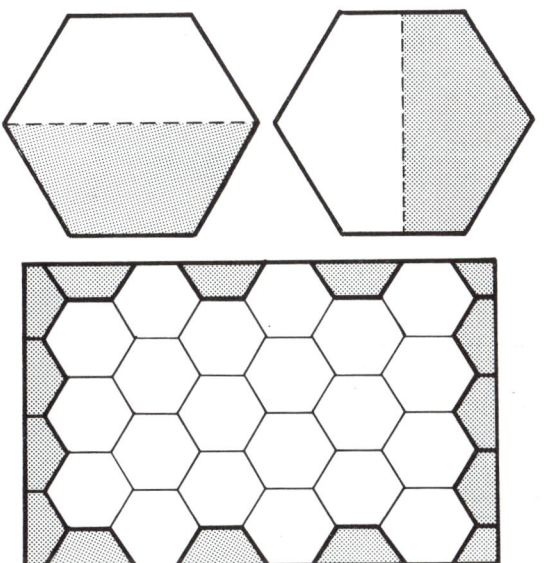

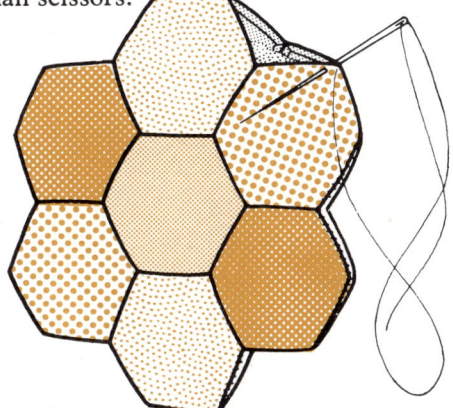

11 Stuff the pincushion firmly with kapok, or old tights or rags cut up into small pieces. Make sure your stuffing is in small pieces rather than large lumps, and press it well down into the corners. Pin the opening and oversew firmly to complete the pincushion.

Other ways of using hexagons

If you decide you would like to make a straight-edged article, such as a cushion cover, from hexagons, cut some of your paper patterns in half in two ways to give you the shapes to make a straight edge.

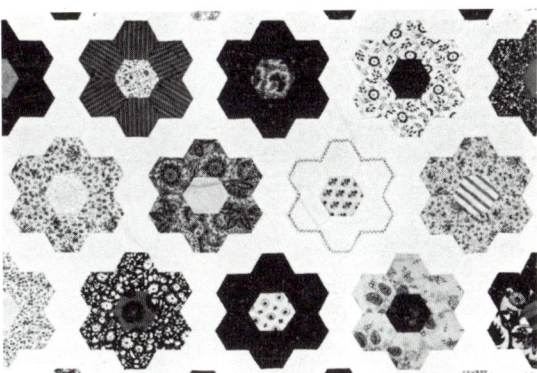

Detail of a quilt made up of brightly coloured rosettes of hexagons set into a background of plain cream hexagons.

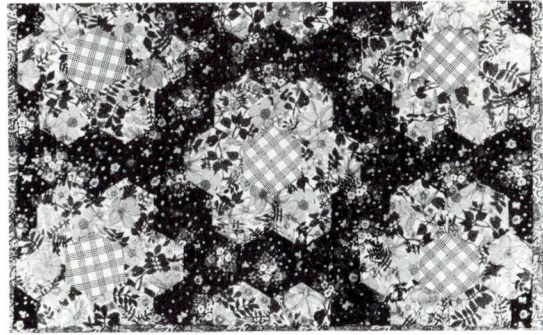

Cot cover in hexagons made from printed lawns.

Two cushions in different versions of the Nine-Patch pattern using printed cottons and cotton lawns. They are easily made up by hand or by machine.

NINE-PATCH CUSHIONS

These two cushions are made up of squares and rectangles. The first one is easily made up by hand without paper patterns, and the second one can be made by machine. It is a good idea to make a diagram of your cushion before you start, colouring in the tones of your chosen fabrics to see if you like the effect.

Hand sewn cushion

This cushion cover is 38 cm (or 15″) square, and you will need a cushion pad about 2.5 cm (1″) larger all round in order to get a nice plump cushion.

```
|<------- 38 cm ------->|
 _____
|       |         |     |
|   a   |    b    |  c  |
|_____|_____|_____|
|       |         |     |
|   d   |    e    |  f  |
|       |         |     |
|_____|_____|_____|
|       |         |     |
|   g   |    h    |  i  |
|_____|_____|_____|
 <-----><--------><----->
  8 cm    22 cm   8 cm
```

1 Make three templates:
a) 8 cm × 8 cm (or 3″ × 3″)
b) 8 cm × 22 cm (or 3″ × 9″)
c) 22 cm × 22 cm (or 9″ × 9″)
(See instructions on page 61.)

2 Now choose your materials. You will need either three blending prints, or three contrasting prints.

3 When you have chosen your materials, wash and iron them before you cut out the patches.

4 On a firm surface and starting with the 8 cm × 8 cm template, place it on the wrong side of the material and draw round the shape with a pencil or fine ball-point pen. Cut out the patch, leaving a seam allowance of 1 cm (or $\frac{3}{8}$″) beyond your drawn line.

5 Cut out three more patches from this template, giving you four altogether. (Patches (a), (c), (g) and (i).)

6 Next, with the 8 cm × 22 cm template, cut out four patches in the same way. (Patches (b), (d), (f) and (h).)

7 With the 22 cm × 22 cm template, cut one patch. (Patch (e).)

8 Arrange your patches on a table or tray to form the nine-patch.

9 To sew up the patches, take pieces (a) and (b) and pin them right sides together along the matched drawn lines. Thread a needle with polyester cotton thread and make a good knot in the end. Make tiny running stitches along the drawn line and finish off with a double stitch. Run the thread back a couple of stitches into the seam allowance for extra strength, then cut the thread.

10 Open out the two patches and press the seam one way, not open.

11 Join (c) to (b) as above to form a strip.

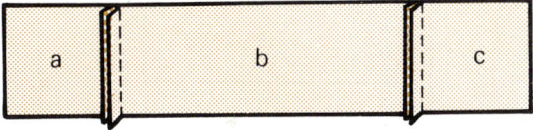

12 Next, join patches (d), (e) and (f).

13 Then join patches (g), (h) and (i). Press all the seams the same way.

14 Take strips (a) (b) (c) and (d) (e) (f) and with right sides together, pin them together along the drawn line. To match the seams exactly, put in a pin along each seam at right angles to the edge.

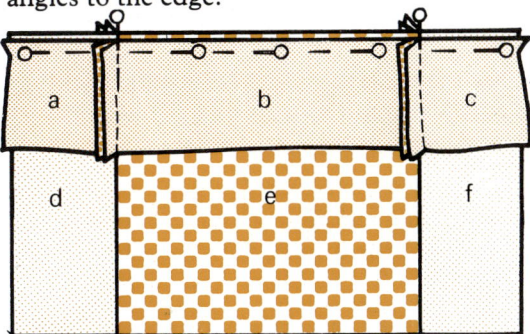

Sew the strips together with tiny running stitches and finish off well. Press the seams one way.

15 Then join strip (g) (h) (i) to (d) (e) (f) in the same way. Press all seams one way and the patchwork is completed.

To make up the cushion cover

1 Take a piece of seam tape 42 cm (or 16″) long (2 cm or ¾″ longer than the side of the patchwork).

2 Pin it to the right side of the patchwork along the top seam allowance.

Either sew it firmly to the patchwork by hand or machine it. Press the tape upwards.

3 Choose a backing for the cushion and cut it 40 cm × 40 cm (or 15½″ × 15½″).

4 Place the backing right sides together with the patchwork and tack around the three untaped edges along the seam line.

5 Machine the three tacked edges carefully. Trim the seam and turn the cover right sides out. Poke out the corners with a small pair of scissors.

6 Put the cushion pad inside the cover. Turn

the top edges of the backing and the seam tape inwards and oversew along the edge.

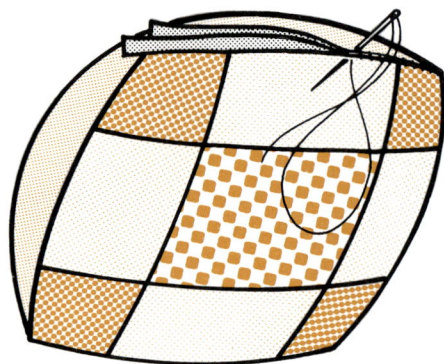

Finish off with a double stitch and take the thread back a few stitches along the edge for extra strength. Cut the thread.

Machine sewn cushion

This cushion cover is 45 cm (or 18″) square, you will need a cushion pad approximately 2.5 cm (1″) larger all round in order to get a nice plump cushion.

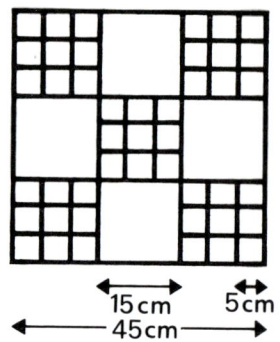

1 Make two templates:
a) 15 cm × 15 cm (or 6″ × 6″)
b) 5 cm × 5 cm (or 2″ × 2″)
(See instructions on page 61.)

2 Now choose your materials with an eye to harmony in the colouring and balance in the size of the prints. You can achieve completely different effects by the way you decide to arrange your materials, as illustrated by the patterns on page 6.

3 When you have chosen your materials, wash and iron them well before you cut out the patches.

4 On a firm surface and starting with the 5 cm × 5 cm template, place it on the wrong side of your material and draw round the shape with a pencil or fine ball-point pen. Cut out the patch leaving a seam allowance of 1 cm (or $\frac{3}{8}''$) beyond your drawn line.

5 Using this template, cut 45 squares altogether from your selection of materials.

6 Next take the 15 cm × 15 cm template and cut four squares in the same way from your chosen materials, with a seam allowance on each one of 1 cm (or $\frac{3}{8}''$).

To make one patched square

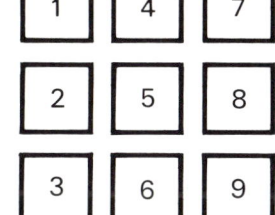

1 Arrange the nine squares in a pretty and harmonious way, balancing tone and contrast in the colours and prints.

2 With right sides together, pin 1 to 2 and 2 to 3, along the matched drawn lines. Machine the two seams and press them open.

3 Repeat for patches 4–5–6 and 7–8–9, so three strips are completed.

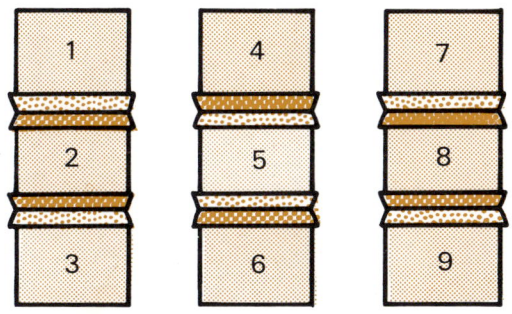

4 To complete the patched square, pin the strips right sides together, matching the seam exactly. To do this, put in a pin into the matched machined seams at right angles to the edge.

Machine the three strips together to form the nine-patch square. Press the seams open. Tie and cut all the threads.

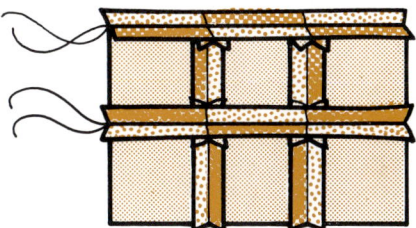

5 Make up the other nine-patch squares in the same way.

6 Arrange the patched squares and the solid squares in their correct positions.

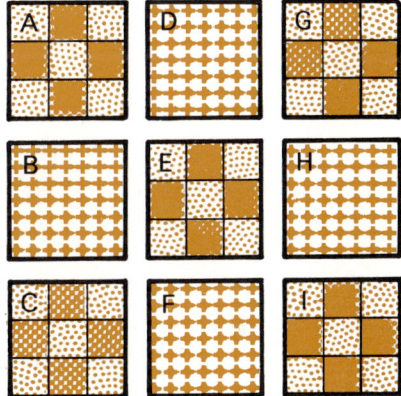

With right sides together, pin A to B and C to B along the matched drawn lines, and machine the seams. Repeat for D–E–F and G–H–I. Press seams open.

7 Pin the three strips right sides together matching the seams accurately. As in (4) above, put pins in at right angles along the seams to be sure of matching them up. Machine the two seams, tie up all threads and cut them off. Press open.

To make up the cushion cover

Follow the instructions for the hand sewn cushion. You will need a piece of seam tape 47 cm (or 19″) long.

Six-pointed stars in a variety of cotton prints can be appliquéd on to shopping bags.

SIX-POINTED STARS

Six-pointed stars, made up of diamonds, are an attractive way to give shopping bags a new look. They can also be appliquéd on to many other things, such as cushions or skirts.
If this is the first time you have used a diamond in patchwork, it is probably easier to assemble them by hand, using paper patterns. The tricky part is to keep the sharp points accurate, but with practice, you will be able to make them up quite easily without papers.

1 To start with, measure the shopping bag and decide on the size of your diamond. For example, if your bag measures 30 cm × 30 cm (approx. 12″ × 12″), you could make diamonds with sides of 7.5 cm (or 3″).

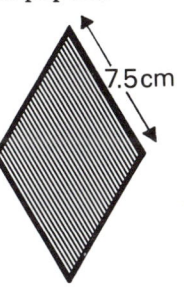

7.5 cm

2 Buy or make a template with sides of your chosen length. (See instructions on page 62.)

3 Use the template to cut out six paper patterns on good quality thick paper, drawing closely round the template with a sharp pencil and cutting accurately along the lines. When you have cut out the papers, check them for accuracy by holding them against your template.

4 Now choose your fabrics. You will need between two and six different prints, depending on the effect you want. Press the fabrics well.

5 Pin the paper patterns to the wrong side of the material and cut the six patches with an allowance of 1 cm (or $\frac{3}{8}$″) all the way round.

6 Thread a needle with tacking cotton but don't knot the thread. Tack the material to the paper by turning it over the edge of the paper. At the sharp corner, fold the material as shown, making sure the material fits snugly

over the paper. Overlap the tacking stitches at the end.

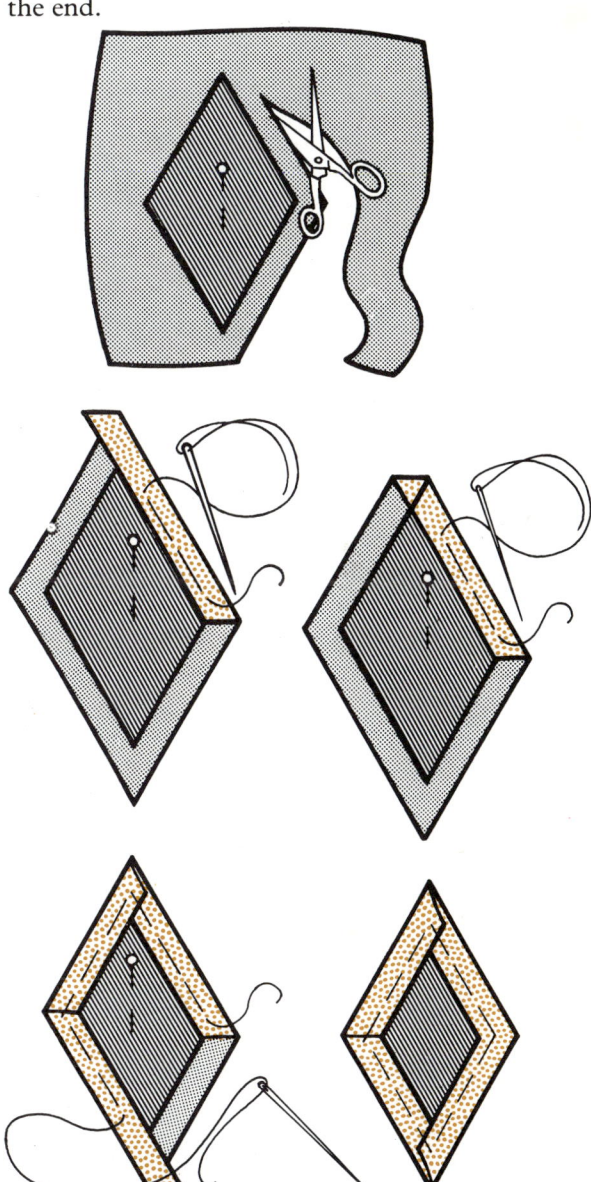

7 When all the patches are tacked, arrange them on a tray or newspaper in your chosen design, balancing colour, tone and size of print.

8 To sew up the patches, thread a No. 8 or No. 9 needle with polyester cotton thread and make a good knot in the end of your thread.

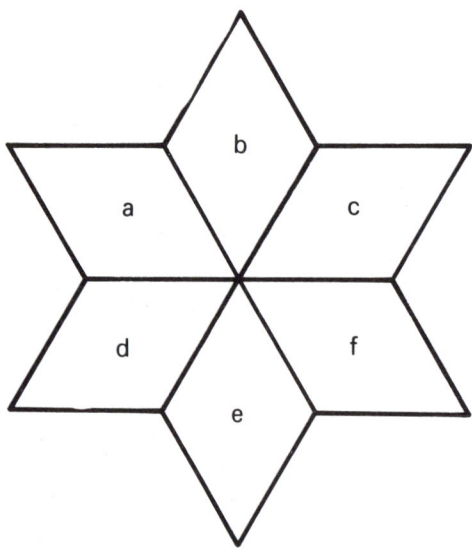

Pick up patches (a) and (b) and place them right sides together exactly on top of each other, making sure the corners match accurately. Put the needle in at the corner A underneath the material and make a double stitch at the corner for strength. Sew with small, firm, even oversewing stitches to join the two edges from A to B, making a double stitch again at the corner B.

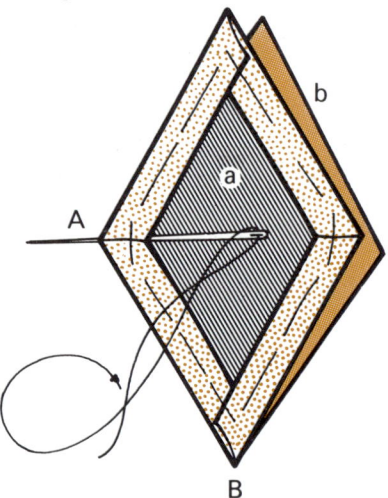

Try not to sew through the paper patterns as these can be used again. Open the two shapes out, take the next patch (c) and place it right sides together with (b). Sew the edges C–D in

the same way, making sure your points meet accurately at D.

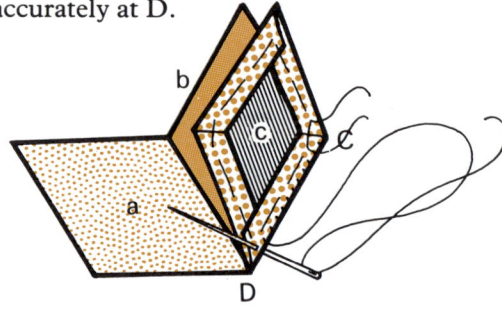

This completes the top half of the star.

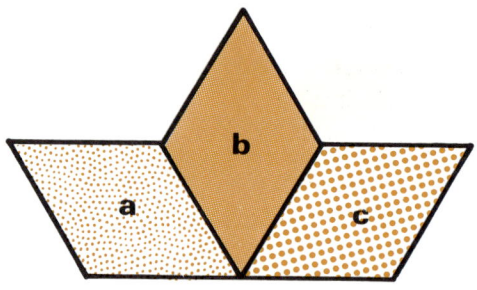

9 Next, sew the three patches (d), (e) and (f) together in the same way.

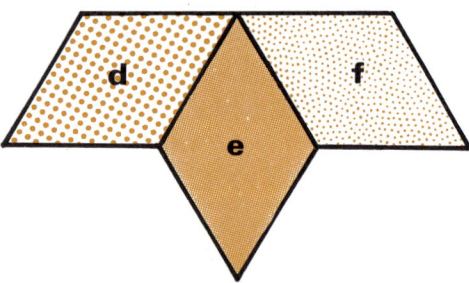

10 Finally, take the two halves of the star and place them right sides together, making sure your central points all meet accurately, otherwise you will end up with a hole in the middle of your star.

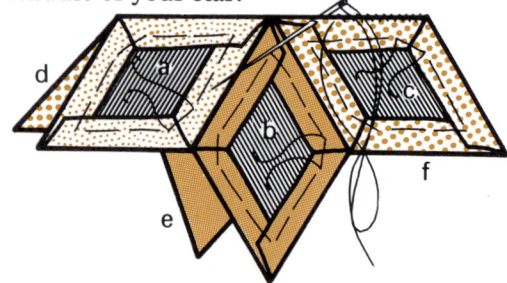

Sew along the central seam with small, even oversewing stitches. Finish with a double stitch and run the thread back into the seam allowance.

To sew the star to the shopping bag

1 Press the star well, then carefully remove the tacking threads and the papers.

2 Tack down the seam allowance around the outside edge of the star. Press again.

3 Make sure the bag is flat and well pressed. Place the star centrally on the bag and pin carefully in place. With the appropriate colour thread, slip stitch around the tacked edge of the star to join it to the bag. Remove the pins and tacking threads and press.

Cushion made up of diamonds arranged in a combination of star shapes and the Baby Blocks pattern.

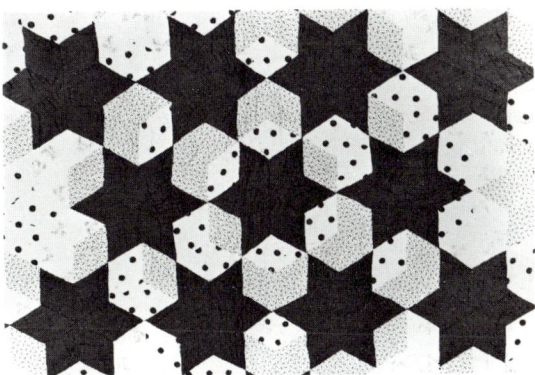

Central medallion of a patchwork bedcover made in Durham around 1870. The six-pointed stars are in a plain red and the surrounding shapes in pale turquoise and cream prints.

These triangles arranged to make different patterns give a new lease of life to a plain curtain, bedspread and apron.

TRIANGLE BORDERS

Borders of patchwork added to already existing plain articles can completely transform their appearance. They can be added to curtains, bedspreads, aprons, skirts or dresses. They can be used to lengthen something or simply to revitalise it. These borders are made up of triangles and are most easily assembled either by hand without papers, or by machine. They are all right-angled triangles (half a square).

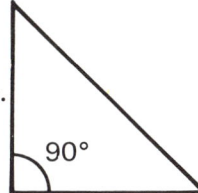

Apron

1 Measure the bottom width of the apron A–B. Then decide how many triangles you would like to see along the bottom. For instance, if the bottom of your apron was 60 cm, you might decide you wanted six triangles, each taking 10 cm of the bottom of the apron, or you might prefer twelve triangles, each taking 5 cm of the bottom of the apron.

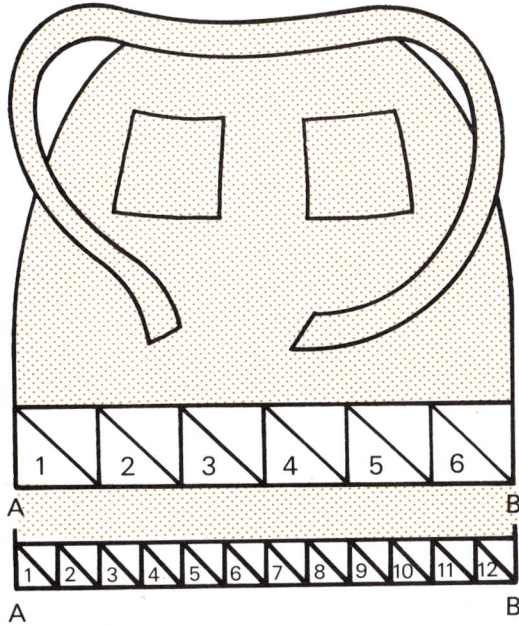

Remember that for each of the two borders you will need to cut twice the number of triangles that make up the width you need.

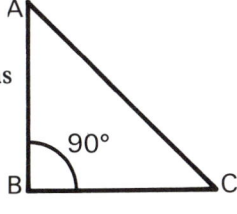

2 Make a template of your chosen size. (See instructions on page 63.)
Sides A–B and B–C should be the same as the length you would like each triangle to take up along the bottom of the apron.

3 Now choose your materials. You will need a selection of prints and plain fabrics, half in light tones, and half in darker tones. Wash and press your fabrics well.

4 Working on a firm surface, place your template on the wrong side of the material, making sure that one side of the triangle is placed along the straight grain of the fabric. Draw round the shape with a pencil or fine ball-point pen. Cut out all your patches, leaving a seam allowance of 1 cm (or $\frac{3}{8}''$) around your drawn line.

5 You can either arrange the triangles on the apron with the dark colours at the bottom and the light colours at the top, to get a saw-tooth effect, or you can arrange your light and dark prints in a more random way. Make sure your prints and colours are well-balanced and harmonized.

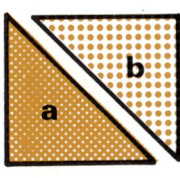

6 To make up the border, start by sewing the triangles into squares.

Take one dark piece (a) and one light piece (b) and pin them right sides together along the matched drawn lines. If you are sewing by hand, thread a No. 8 or No. 9 needle with polyester cotton thread and make a good knot in the end. Make tiny running stitches along the drawn line and finish off with a double

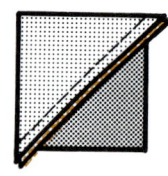

stitch. Run the thread back into the seam allowance for extra security. Press the seam one way, towards the darker fabric. If you are machining the patches, press the seams open.

7 When all your squares are completed, line them up with all the dark triangles at the bottom and pin them right sides together along the drawn lines. Sew the seams using the same technique as you used for sewing up the squares.

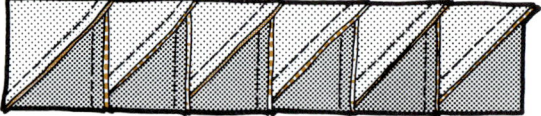

Press well, and the first border is completed.

8 Make up the second border in the same way, arranging your patches in a different order.

To attach the borders to the apron

1 Decide on the position of the first border on the apron. Pin the top edge of the border right sides together with the apron, making sure it is parallel with the hem.

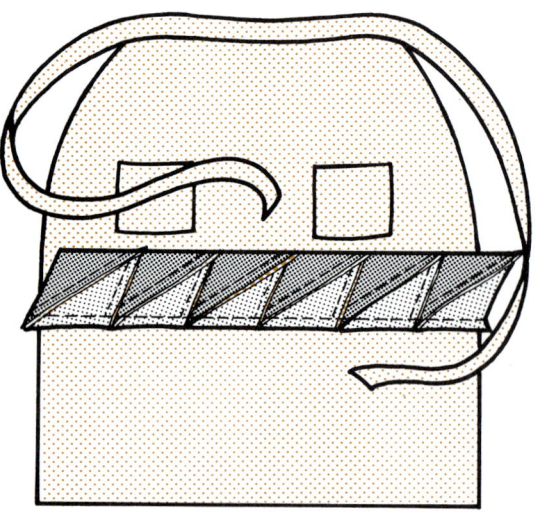

Either machine the seam or sew with small running stitches, taking the thread back a couple of stitches into the seam allowance for extra security. Press the border downwards.

2 Turn in the seam allowance on both sides and the bottom edge of the border and pin to the apron. Either machine round the border or slip stitch to the apron.

3 Attach the second border in the same way to the bottom of the apron.

Press the apron well.

Bedspread

1 Measure all four edges of the bedspread and decide how many triangles you would like round the edge, as for the apron. (See note **1** on page 23.) Remember you will need to cut twice this number of triangles for the border.

2 Make a template of your chosen size (see instructions on page 61).

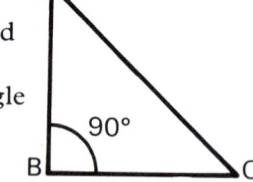

Sides A–B and B–C should be the same as the length you would like each triangle to take up along the edge of the bedspread.

3 Now choose your materials. You will need two prints, one dark and one light, to harmonize with the bedspread and the bedroom. Wash and press the fabrics well.

4 To make up the border, cut out all your patches, half in the dark print and half in the light, following the instructions given for the apron. (See notes **4** and **6** on page 23.)

5 When all your squares are completed, line them up with the dark squares alternating at the top and bottom, and sew them together along your drawn lines. Press well. Make up the two sides and top and bottom borders separately.

Arrange the squares at the corners like this:

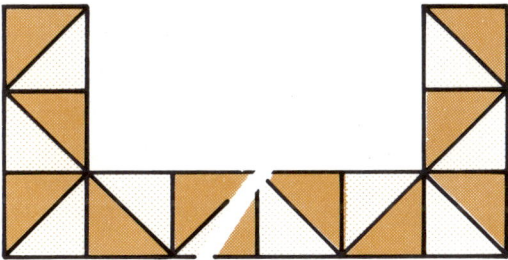

Press well and the borders are completed.

To attach the borders to the bedspread

1 Sew the borders to the sides of the bedspread first, in your chosen position, making sure the border is parallel with the hem of the bedspread. Follow the instructions given for the apron. (See facing page.)

2 Attach the borders at the top and bottom in the same way, slip stitching together the triangles at the corners where the two sides meet. Press well.

Curtains

1 Measure the bottom width of your curtains and decide how many triangles you would like to see along the bottom. (See note **1** on page 23.)

2 Make a template of your chosen size (see instructions on page 61).

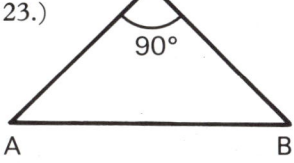

Sides A–B should be the same length as you would like each triangle to take up along the bottom of the curtains.

3 Now choose your materials. You will need two prints, one dark and one light, to harmonize with the curtains and the room in which they are going.

4 This border is made up of a double row of triangles arranged to make a zig-zag pattern.

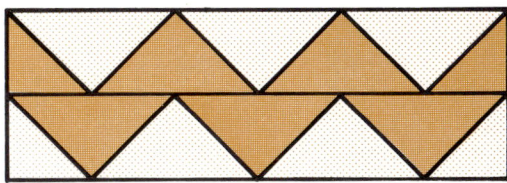

For each half of the border, you will need to cut twice the number of triangles you decided you would need along the bottom of the curtains.

5 Cut out the patches, half in the dark print and half in the light, following the instructions given for the apron. (See note **4** on page 23.)

6 Make up each half of the border separately. Arrange the triangles, alternating light and dark, and pin right sides together along the matched drawn lines. Machine the seams. Continue until you have completed both halves of the border. Press well.

7 Arrange the two halves of the border to form a zig-zag pattern and pin the centre seam.

Check that your pattern is correctly lined up. Tack the seam and machine. Tie and cut the threads and press the border well.

Attach the border to the curtain in the same way as for the apron.

Four Log Cabin squares arranged with the light sides towards the centre make this simple, fresh-looking cushion.

LOG CABIN CUSHION

Log Cabin is an interesting form of patchwork and the only one in this book for which you do not need a template. The pattern has been used both in this country and in America, and the English examples are also known as Log Wood or Ribbon patchwork. The fabrics are divided into light and dark shades, cut into strips and sewn around a central square to form a larger square. The arrangement of dark strips on one side of the central patch and light on the other has given rise to a tradition that the central patch represents the hearth, and the light and dark sides are the firelight and shadow. The finished squares can be arranged in a number of ways and many arrangements have traditional names, such as Straight Furrow or Barnraising (see p. 60). This cushion is made up of four squares, arranged with the light sides of the squares towards the centre. It is made by machine but can also be hand sewn.

1 Decide on the width of strip you want, according to the measurement of your finished block. The actual measurement is not vitally important since you can increase the size of your square simply by adding more strips. However, it is better not to make them too narrow. Perhaps you will find the width of a ruler or metre stick is right, or you could make a strip of card to use as a guide when cutting the material.

2 Now choose your fabrics – you could use all plains or all prints, or a mixture of both. You can use any number from two upwards, but they must be equal numbers of light and dark. Sometimes the central square is one completely different contrasting colour. If you are using striped material, cut it with the stripes going across the width of the strip. One slight variation in the straightness of your seam with stripes going along the length of the strip may give the patchwork an uneven look.

3 Using your ruler or width guide, mark out with a pencil or fine ball-point pen long strips on the wrong side of the material, along the straight grain. Don't worry about the length of the strips at this stage. Leave a seam allowance of 1 cm (or $\frac{3}{8}$") on either side of your strips and cut equal numbers of strips from your dark and light fabrics. It is very important that the width should be consistently accurate.

4 Take one light strip A and one dark strip B and pin, right sides together, along the drawn line on A. Sew the two strips together right across the width of strip B.

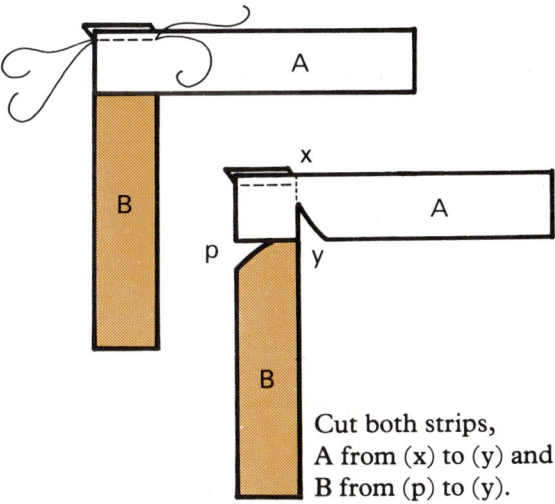

Cut both strips, A from (x) to (y) and B from (p) to (y).

You know have a small strip made up of one square of light and one square of dark fabric. Press the seam one way.

Take a dark strip and pin right sides together from (a) to (b). Machine the seam along the

27

drawn line and through the seam allowances, and cut the strip off at (x)–(y).

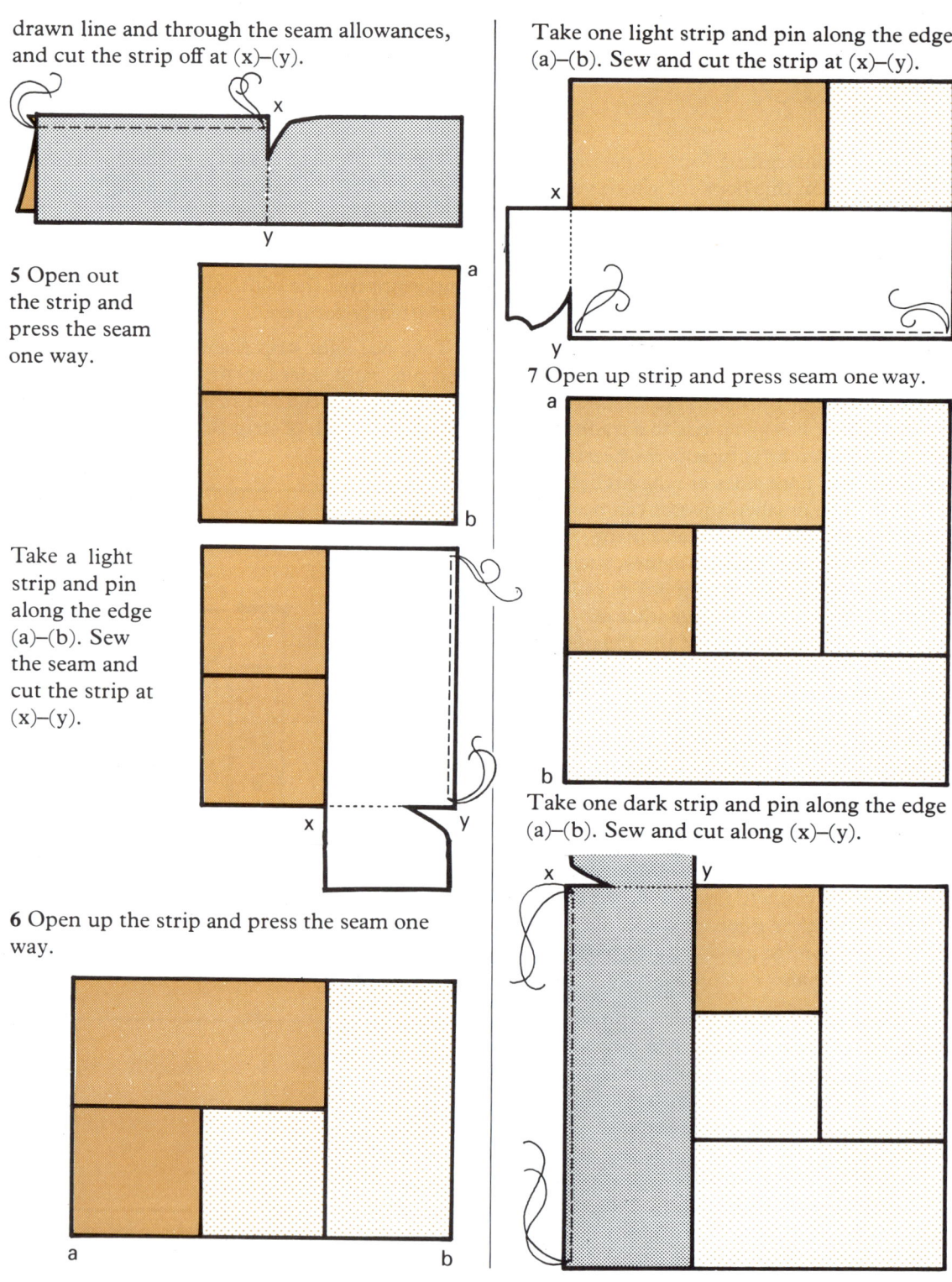

5 Open out the strip and press the seam one way.

Take a light strip and pin along the edge (a)–(b). Sew the seam and cut the strip at (x)–(y).

6 Open up the strip and press the seam one way.

Take one light strip and pin along the edge (a)–(b). Sew and cut the strip at (x)–(y).

7 Open up strip and press seam one way.

Take one dark strip and pin along the edge (a)–(b). Sew and cut along (x)–(y).

8 Open up the strip and press the seam one way.

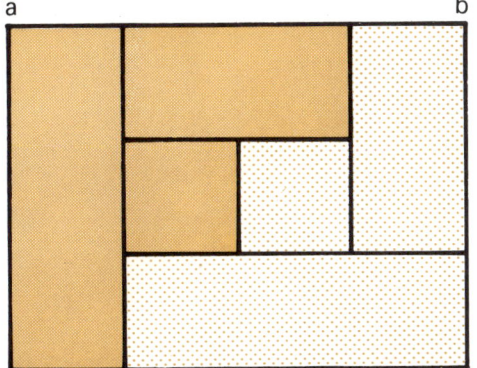

Take one dark strip and pin along the edge (a)–(b). Sew and cut along (x)–(y).

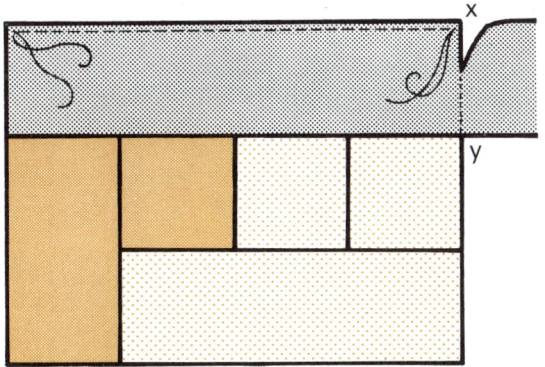

9 Open up the strip and press the seam one way.

Continue in a clockwise direction, sewing two light strips, then two dark strips until you reach the size square you want. Sew the next strip on this square along (a)–(b). Then sew a light strip along (b)–(c). Then a dark strip along (c)–(d) and a dark strip along (d)–(a). Press the square well.

10 This cushion has two extra dark strips which form the border when the four squares are sewn together.

11 Make three more squares in the same way, mixing your prints differently, but keeping the light/dark contrast.

12 To make up the cover, arrange your four squares with the light sides towards the centre. Place the top two squares right sides together. Pin and machine along the matched drawn lines. Then sew the bottom two squares together in the same way. Press well and join the two halves right sides together along the centre seam, making sure that the central meeting point is accurate.

You can either make the back of the cushion in the same way, or use a piece of plain fabric. Make up the cover according to the instructions on page 16.

For more examples of Log Cabin arrangements, see page 60.

One Log Cabin rectangle makes an original idea for a work bag.

This simple waistcoat in toning browns is made of square patches set diagonally to form diamonds.

PATCHWORK WAISTCOAT

Patchwork can be used very effectively in the wardrobe, either to create complete garments or to revitalise and alter old ones. The important thing is to stick to simple shapes and simple patterns.

This waistcoat is made up of squares set diagonally to form diamonds, in four toning fabrics. It is better to make up the area of patchwork first and then cut out your pattern from it. The pattern will fit a 34″–36″ bust. Reduce or enlarge it accordingly if necessary. The amount of patchwork needed for this waistcoat is quickly assembled by machine.

1 Decide on the weight of material and the colour scheme that you want. Choose four materials (in the illustration there are three prints and a blending plain colour). Wash and press them well. (You *can* use any number of blending materials and vary your method accordingly.) Number the materials 1, 2, 3 and 4.

2 Buy or make a square template with sides of 7 cm (or 2¾″). (See instructions on page 61.)

3 Working on a hard surface, place the template on the wrong side of the fabric and mark round the edge with a pencil or fine ball-point pen, making sure that the template is on the straight grain of the fabric. Cut with an allowance of 1 cm (or ⅜″). You will need 30 squares of each material (120 in all).

4 To make up a length of material of squares set into a diamond pattern, you will make up 15 strips of two sorts: one using fabrics 1 and 2, and one using fabrics 3 and 4. The strips vary in length (see pattern on the next two pages): the first uses two squares of 1 and 2, the second four squares of 3 and 4, the third six squares of 1 and 2, the fourth eight squares of 3 and 4 and so on, following the pattern.

You will end up with a finished area measuring 100 cm × 48 cm which you will fold along the length to measure 50 cm × 48 cm when you cut out the pattern.

5 Make up all your strips by putting the squares right sides together, matching the drawn lines. Pin and machine along the line. Press the seams open.

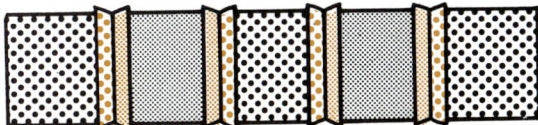

6 Lay your well-pressed completed strips out on a table, according to the pattern. Join them all together, starting by placing strip (1) right sides together with strip (2) (see diagram). Match the drawn lines, pin and put extra pins at right angles into the matched seams. Machine and press the seam open. Repeat for strip (3) etc. until all the strips are joined to form a rectangular area. Press well.

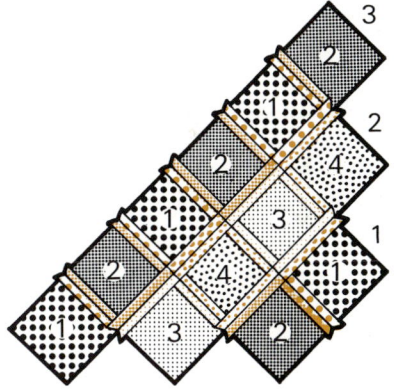

To make the pattern

1 Take a sheet of brown paper and measure out an area 50 cm × 48 cm (or 19¾″ × 19″).

2 Mark the grid of squares as indicated in the pattern by marking off 10 cm points (or 4″) along all four edges and joining the opposite points to make up the grid.

3 Following the diagram, mark off the pattern matching the points where the lines of the pattern cross the lines of the grid.

4 Cut out the pattern, adding a seam allowance of 1 cm (or $\frac{3}{8}''$).

To make up the waistcoat

1 Fold the patchwork half way along the length and place the centre back of the pattern to the fold. Pin well through both layers and cut with a seam allowance of 1 cm ($\frac{3}{8}''$).

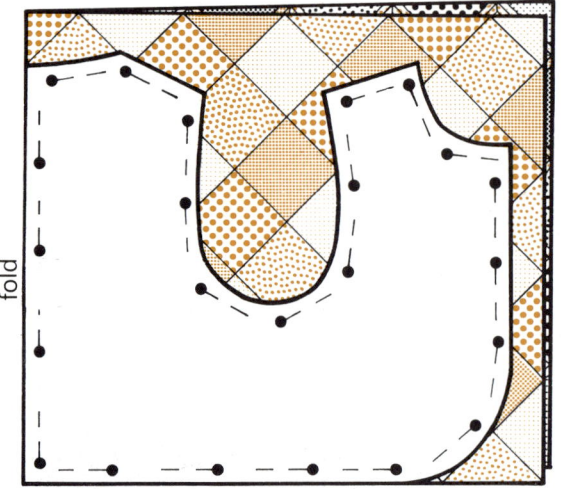

2 Choose a suitable weight and colour lining fabric and cut as for the patchwork side. Press.

3 Pin the lining and the patchwork *wrong sides together* from the centre back outwards to ensure flatness.

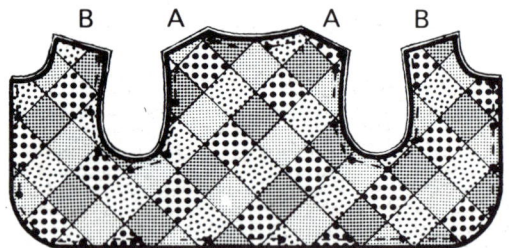

Sew the shoulder seams of the patchwork only by placing A and B right sides together. Pin

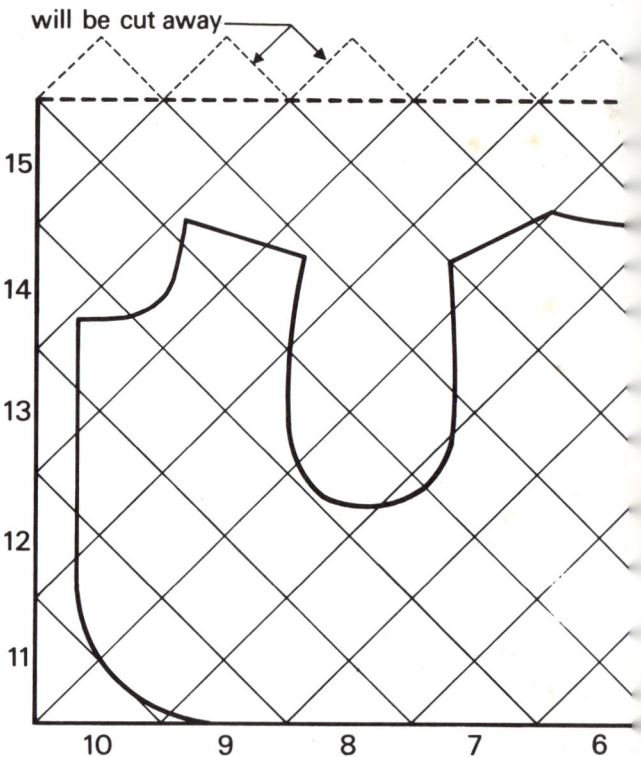

and machine along the seam allowance. Press the seam open. Turn the edges of the shoulder seams of the lining inwards and slip stitch.

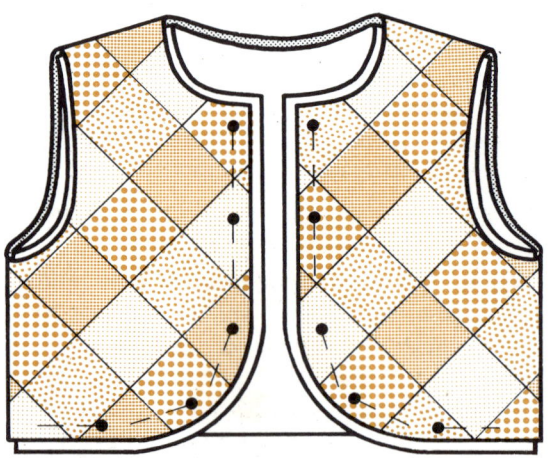

4 To finish off the outside edges, cut long bias strips of your chosen colour 2.5 cm (or 1")

strip 5   strip 4   strip 3   strip 2   strip 1

wide and join them together to make very long strips:

one strip for the neck edge and ties 115 cm (or 45″)

two strips for the armholes 48 cm each (or 19″)

one strip for the outside edge 146 cm (or 58″)

5 Bind all the edges by placing the seam allowance of the bias strip (0.5 mm or $\frac{1}{4}$″) along the seam allowance on the right side of the patchwork. Pin, tack and machine.

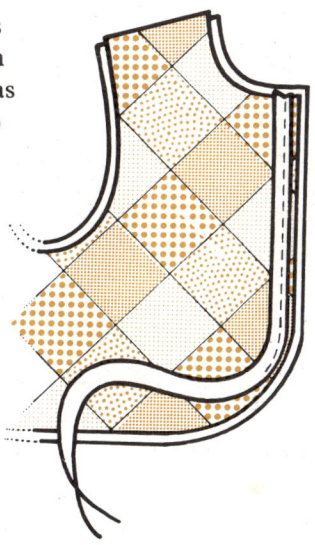

At the neck edge, leave about 33 cm on each side (or 13″) at the centre front to make the two ties.

6 Trim the edges of the waistcoat and lining and turn the binding to the wrong side. Pin all round and slip stitch to the lining. For the ties, fold the two lengths at the neck in half lengthwise, turn the edges under at the seam allowance and slip stitch the edges together, turning in the ends.

Patchwork squares in different shades of purple are used to lengthen this velvet skirt.

This cushion is made up of one block of the pattern called Jacob's Ladder.

JACOB'S LADDER CUSHION

This cushion is made up in the pattern called Jacob's Ladder. It is one of the numerous American block patterns which are characteristic of their patchwork. The blocks, many of which have intriguing names, make ideal patterns for cushions and there is a further selection to choose from on pages 59 and 60. Get into the habit of determining the form of the block – many of them divide up into a four-patch or a nine-patch block. Jacob's Ladder is a nine-patch pattern.

The block pattern is wherever possible sewn up with straight seams – it is broken down into sections, the sections then sewn into strips and finally the strips sewn together to complete the block. This made them quick to construct and consequently they were frequently used to make up quilts. The block also had the advantage of being easier to handle than a whole quilt in the often cramped kitchens of rural homes. The blocks were sewn by hand without paper patterns and when the sewing machine came into general use in the 1880s, this increased the speed and ease of construction.

It is a good idea to draw your block out first and mark in your chosen colours to see if you like the effect.

This block is 30 cm × 30 cm (or 12″ × 12″) and we have added a 5 cm (or 2″) border. You will need a cushion pad approximately 2.5 cm (or 1″) larger all round than your finished square of patchwork. It can be sewn by hand without paper patterns or by machine. When machining, press the seams open and not one way as with hand-stitching.

1 Make two templates
a) a square 5 cm × 5 cm (or 2″ × 2″)
b) a right-angled triangle whose equal sides are 10 cm (or 4″) (see instructions on page 61 and 63).

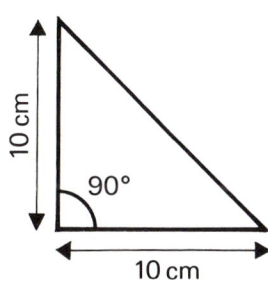

2 Choose three fabrics which go well together in light, medium and darker tones. Wash and press them well.

3 You will need
10 squares of the dark fabric
10 squares of the light fabric
4 triangles of the medium fabric
4 triangles of the light fabric.

Place the template on the wrong side of the fabric and draw around the edge with a pencil or fine ball-point pen. Cut the patches leaving an allowance of 1 cm (or $\frac{3}{8}$″) beyond your drawn line.

4 Arrange your patches on a tray or sheet of newspaper in the Jacob's Ladder design. Then sort them out into the order for sewing. The nine squares are sewn up separately, then into strips of three, then the three strips into the final block.

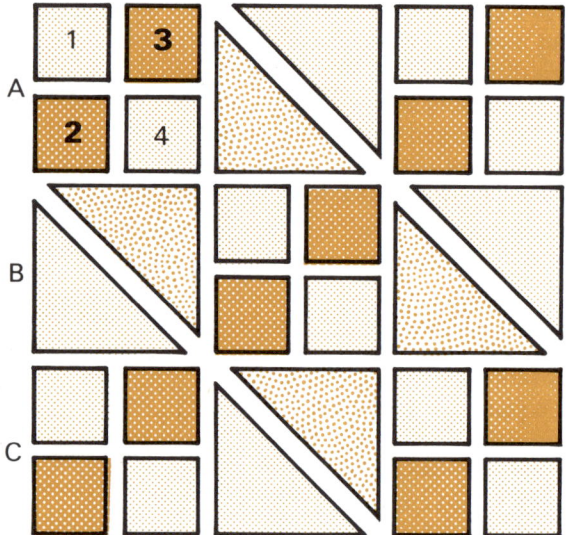

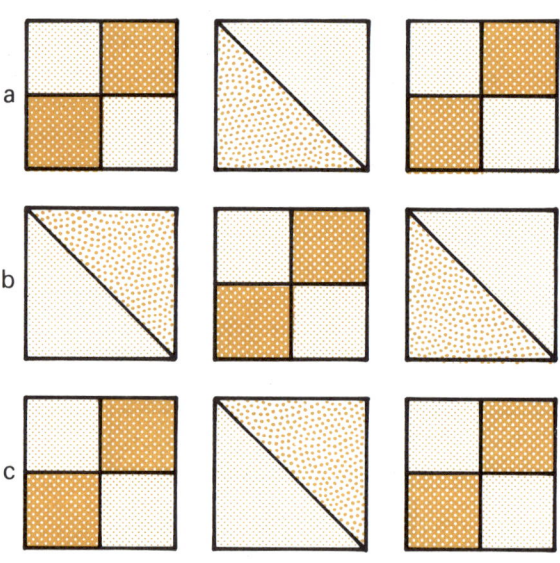

Continue until all nine squares are complete.

7 The next stage is to sew up the squares into three strips.

5 Starting with square A, place sections 1 and 2 right sides together making sure both drawn lines are matched. Thread a No. 8 or 9 needle with polyester cotton thread and make a good knot in the end. Sew with small, regular running stitches through the seam allowances along the drawn line. Finish with a double stitch and run the thread back into the seam allowance for extra strength. Press the seam one way. Sew sections 3 and 4 together in the same way.

Place square (a) right sides together with square (b), match up the drawn lines and pin. Sew the seam. Then sew square (c) right sides together with (b). Press the seams one way. Repeat for the remaining two strips.

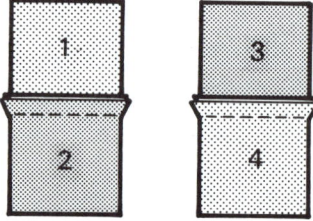

Pin the two strips right sides together, matching the central seam and sew up along the matched drawn lines. Press the seam one way. This completes the first of the nine squares of which this pattern is composed.

6 For square B, place the two triangles right sides together and sew up along the matched drawn lines. Press the seam one way.

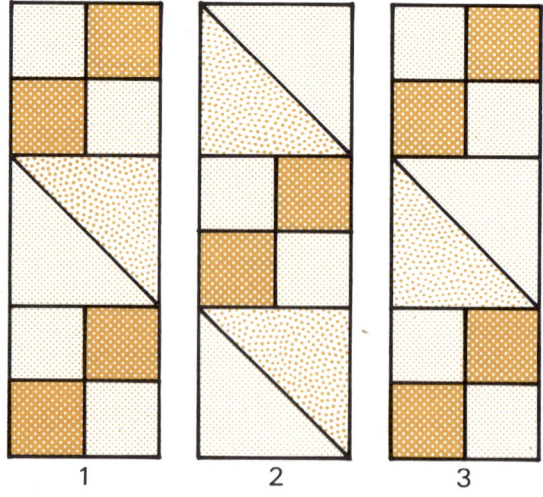

Then sew the three strips together by placing strips 1 and 2 right sides together, pinning carefully along the drawn lines and matching the seams exactly. Repeat for 2 and 3. Press the block well.

Border

1 Choose a contrasting or blending print and cut
two strips 7 cm × 30 cm (or $2\frac{3}{4}'' \times 12''$)
two strips 7 cm × 46 cm (or $2\frac{3}{4}'' \times 18''$)
2 Join the two 7 cm × 30 cm strips to each side of your block, allowing 1 cm on the border for the seam.

Join the longer strips to the top and bottom and stitch in the same way. Press well.

Make up the cover following the instructions on page 16.

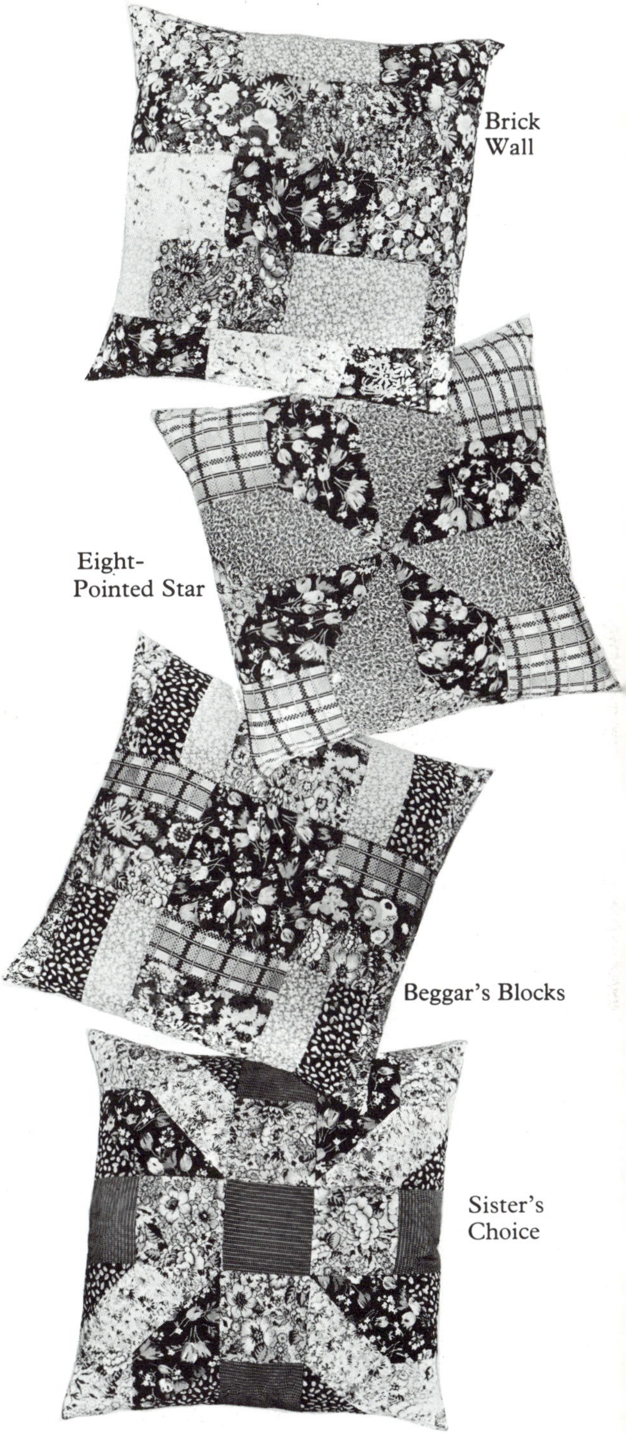

Brick Wall

Eight-Pointed Star

Beggar's Blocks

Sister's Choice

Here are four more examples of cushions made up of one block pattern. The materials are toning prints in creams, blues, reds and purples.

This bedcover was made in America around 1870. The pattern is called Square in the Middle and it is made from blue and white spotted cottons.

Inset Detail showing the construction of two blocks.

SQUARE IN THE MIDDLE BED COVER

Once you have practised a number of block patterns, you will probably like to tackle the larger task of making a bed cover. Choosing a pattern for your blocks is only the first of a number of decisions you will have to make: how big the cover should be and how many blocks you will need; have you enough material in your chosen colours to complete the cover; do you want a border round the cover and how are you going to join your blocks together?

This cover, which was made in America around 1870, is based on two simple blocks, each of which uses the same two fabrics. One block is a nine-patch and the other a square surrounded by triangles. Together, they give the effect of a square set diagonally surrounded by a chain of smaller squares. The pattern has vitality and freshness and it is well within the reach of the newcomer to patchwork.

Joining the blocks together is known as setting. These blocks have been joined side by side to create an overall design. There are two other frequently used ways of setting blocks: the first is to divide your blocks with lattice strips of material; the second is to alternate patched and solid squares. They do, of course, cut down on the number of patched blocks you will have to make but your considerations for deciding which form to use should be artistic rather than labour-saving! It is a good idea to draw your block on paper first, then draw a group of four together – look at it carefully and decide whether they work set side by side or whether it would be better to separate them.

As all the seams in this pattern are straight, it is easy to make by machine.

Blocks separated by lattice strips.

Blocks set diagonally separated by solid squares.

1 Measure your bed and its overhang at the sides and bottom and decide on the size of your cover. Draw a scale diagram and work out how many blocks fit into your chosen size. A block can be any size, but if they are too small the design can look fussy and if they're too big, you lose the proportions of the pattern. The best sizes are probably between 20 cm and 30 cm square (or between 8″ and 12″ square).

2 The two blocks which make up this cover are 21 cm square (or 9″ square).

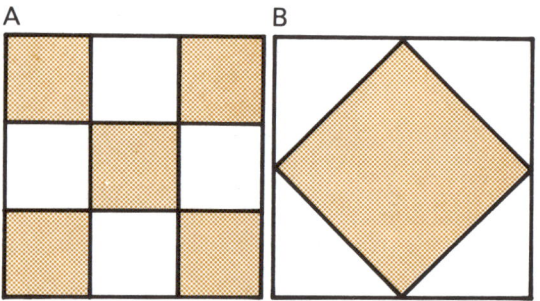

A   B

You will need two fabrics, blue and white. These old fabrics are delicately spotted but the cover would be just as effective in plain colours.

3 Make three templates (see instructions on page 61).

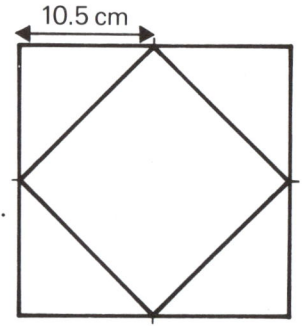

10.5 cm

For Block A, a square 7 cm × 7 cm (or 3″ × 3″). For Block B, make a square 21 cm × 21 cm (or 9″ × 9″). Along each side of the square mark off 10.5 cm (or 4½″). Join the four points. Cut along the drawn lines. This will give you a square and a right-angled triangle whose equal sides are 10.5 cm (or 4½″). Make several of each shape before you begin to cut your patches. Check that they are all accurate.

4 Wash and press your fabrics well. Working on a hard surface, place your templates on the wrong side of the material and draw round the shapes with a sharp pencil or fine ball-point pen. Cut leaving a seam allowance of 1 cm (or ⅜″) round each patch.

To sew up

1 Block A Arrange the squares in the correct way for the design.

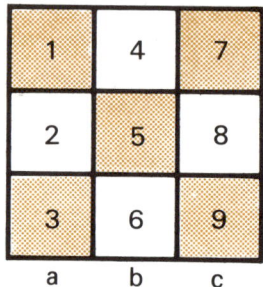

1	4	7
2	5	8
3	6	9

a   b   c

Place patches 1 and 2 right sides together, pin and machine along drawn line. Sew 3 to 2 in the same way to complete the strip. Repeat for patches 4, 5 and 6 and 7, 8 and 9 and press the seams open.

To complete the patched square, pin strip (a) right sides together with (b), and (c) right sides together with (b), matching the seams exactly by putting in a pin at right angles to the edge into the seams.

Machine the three strips together to form the nine-patch square. Press the seams open and tie up the threads. Block A is completed. Make as many blocks as you require for your cover.

2 Block B Arrange the patches in the correct way for the design.

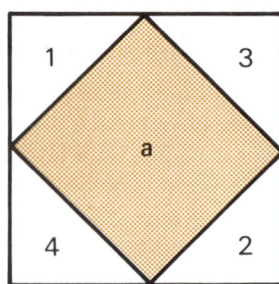

1		3
	a	
4		2

Place patch 1 right sides together with (a) and sew along the drawn line. Place patch 2 right sides together with (a) as indicated and sew

along the drawn line.
At this stage it is very
important to press
the two triangles flat
with the seams open
before you sew on
the last two.
Then join patches 3 and
4 to (a) in the same way.
Press again. Block B is
completed. Make as many blocks
as you require for your coverlet.

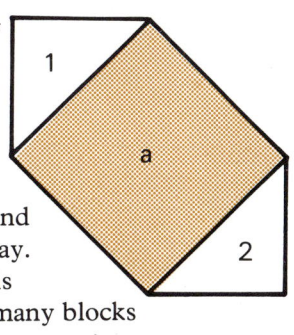

To stitch the blocks together

1 Place Block A right sides together with
Block B and match up the drawn lines. Pin
and sew. Press the seams open. Build up an
area of blocks working in strips which you
then sew together.

When joining the strips together, match the
seams accurately by putting in a pin at right
angles to the seams.

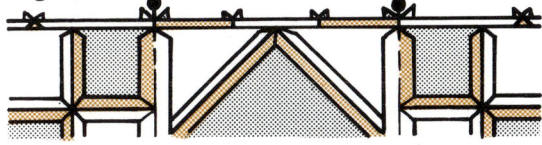

Press well as you go along. When you have
joined all your blocks together, the cover is
ready for lining.

To line the cover

1 Choose a suitable weight and colour fabric
(a heavy cotton or calico). Cut to the same size
as your cover, joining if necessary with a seam
down the middle.

2 Place the lining and the patched top *wrong
sides together* and pin together, working from
the centre outwards to the edges to ensure the
cover will lie flat. There are a number of ways
of finishing off the edge of the cover.

i) Turn the seam allowance of the two layers
inwards, pin together in a straight line and
slip stitch the two layers together all the way
round. Press well.

ii) Cut long strips from either material and
bind the edges.

iii) Make a border from either of the fabrics
and sew first to the top and bottom and then
to the two sides of your patched area, in the
same way as for the Jacob's Ladder cushion
(see page 37). Cut your lining large enough to
include the border and either finish off as for
(i) or bind the edges.

A patchwork cover is more than just a bed
covering. You can stitch aspects of your life
into a cover which produces something for
family and home which can be passed on from
one generation to the next. You could
revive the old tradition of the Friendship
Quilt, either by begging enough material from
each of your friends to make up one block, or
by holding a party and asking your friends to
come with their material and make up the
blocks themselves, each one different.

A great grandmother of Ohio described her
feelings about a cover she made for her
family: 'It took me more than twenty years,
nearly twenty-five, I reckon, in the evenings
after supper when the children were all put to
bed. My whole life is in that quilt. It scares me
sometimes when I look at it. All my joys and
all my sorrows are stitched into those little
pieces. When I was proud of the boys and
when I was downright provoked and angry
with them. When the girls annoyed me or
when they gave me a warm feeling around my
heart. And John too. He was stitched into that
quilt and all the thirty years we were married.
Sometimes I loved him and sometimes I sat
there hating him as I pieced the patches
together. So they are all in that quilt, my
hopes and fears, my joys and sorrows, my
loves and hates. I tremble sometimes when I
remember what that quilt knows about me.'

The Star of Bethlehem pattern with a border of squares makes up this striking floor cushion.

STAR OF BETHLEHEM FLOOR CUSHION

The Star of Bethlehem is an eight-pointed star, made up of long diamonds. On this floor cushion, the star is made up into a square by adding squares and triangles round the outside edges, and the border is made up of squares. It is a good idea to make a drawing before you begin with the measurements of the patches and your proposed colour scheme marked on it. The instructions in this chapter are based on a cushion pad 90 cm × 90 cm (or 36″ × 36″). If you prefer to use a different size, work out the width of the border and the size of star required to fit your pad.

The instructions are given for sewing by machine, but it can be sewn by hand, with or without paper patterns, if preferred. (See instructions for using paper patterns on p. 19.)

To make the star

1 Buy or make a long diamond template with sides of 5 cm (or 2″). (See instructions on page 63.)

2 Now choose your fabrics. You will need five prints – two dark, two medium and one light. Wash and press them well.

3 Each segment of the star is made up separately and the eight segments are then joined together.
To make up the patches for the first segment, place your template on the wrong side of the material pressing on a hard surface and mark round the shape with a pencil or fine ball-point pen. Leaving a seam allowance of 1 cm (or ⅜″) outside your drawn line, cut:
five patches from the light print
two patches from the first medium print
three patches from the second medium print
four patches from the first dark print
two patches from the second dark print.

You will have a total of 16 diamonds for each segment (128 in all).

4 Arrange your diamonds on a tray or newspaper in the following order:

1st medium print

light print

2nd medium print

1st dark print

light print

2nd dark print

1st medium print

5 To sew up, take patches 1 and 2, place right sides together and machine through the seam allowances along the matched drawn lines. Sew patches 2 to 3 and 3 to 4, so that strip A is completed. Press seams one way towards the outside edge.

6 Sew the other three strips B, C and D in the same way.

For strip B, join patches 5, 6, 7 and 8.
For strip C, join patches 9, 10, 11 and 12.
For strip D, join patches 13, 14, 15 and 16.
Tie and cut threads and press all the seams one way, towards the outside edge.

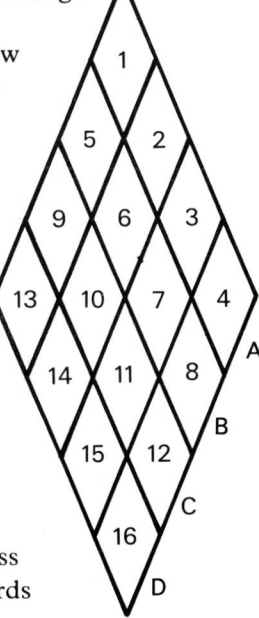

7 To join the strips to form the first segment of the star, pin strip A right sides together with strip B. Match the seams exactly by putting in a pin at right angles to the stitching into the seams.

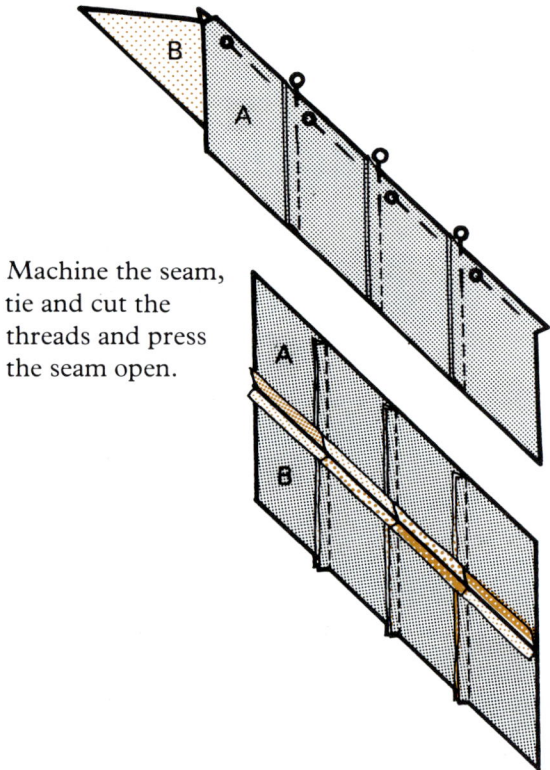

Machine the seam, tie and cut the threads and press the seam open.

8 Sew strip B to C and C to D in the same way and the first segment is complete.

9 Make up the other seven segments in exactly the same way, arranging your prints in the same order as for the first segment.

10 You are now ready to sew the segments together to make the star. It is essential to match the seams very accurately, as the centre is the meeting point for eight sharp angles.

Place two segments right sides together and pin carefully, matching the seams by putting a pin at right angles into the matched seams. Start sewing at point (a) at the beginning of your drawn line, not at the edge of the material, and sew to point (b), through the seam allowance to the edge of the material. By

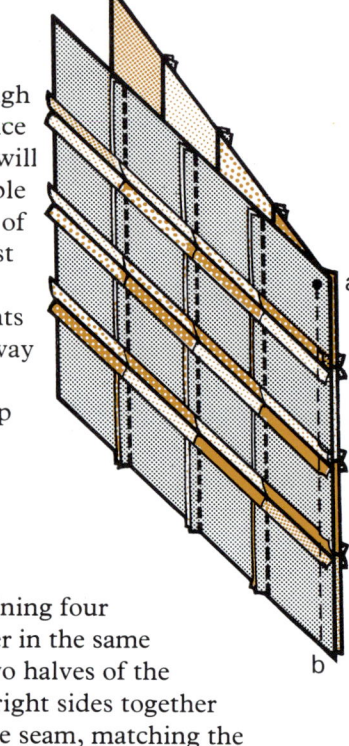

not sewing through the seam allowance at point (a), you will more easily be able to join the edges of the star to the rest of the shapes. Join four segments together in this way until you have completed the top half of the star.

11 Join the remaining four segments together in the same way. Take the two halves of the star, place them right sides together and pin the centre seam, matching the centre point accurately.

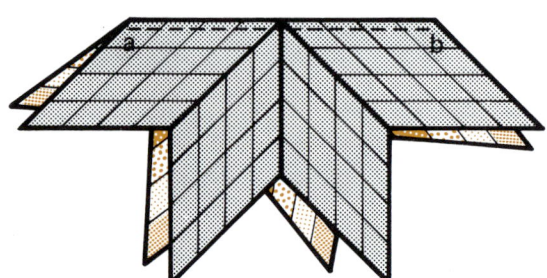

Sew the centre seam from point (a) to point (b) along the drawn line, but not through the seam allowance. Tie and cut threads and press the star.

To make up the star into a square

1 Make two templates (see instructions on page 61 and 63):
a) a square 20 cm × 20 cm (or 8″ × 8″)
b) a right angle triangle whose equal sides are 20 cm (or 8″) (half the square).

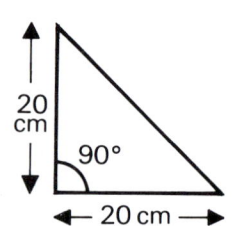

2 Using your second dark print, cut four squares and four triangles, by placing your templates on the wrong side of the material, and drawing round the edge with a sharp pencil or ball-point pen. Cut the patches with a seam allowance of 1 cm (or $\frac{3}{8}''$).

3 Place one side of a square along one side of a star point, right sides together and pin. Match the corners accurately and sew from (a) through the seam allowance to (b), at the end of the drawn line.

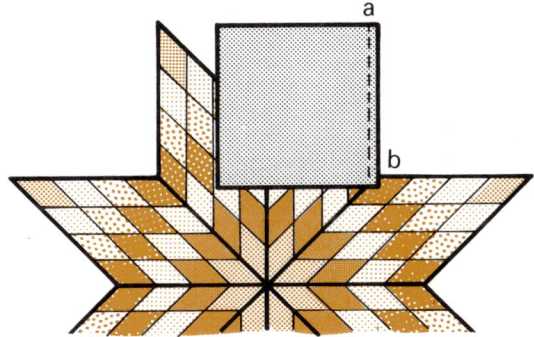

Ease the square round and pin the second side to the adjacent point of the star, and sew along the drawn line to the edge of the material. Press seams outwards. Continue round the star, alternating squares and triangles, until you have a square 70 cm × 70 cm (or $27\frac{1}{2}'' \times 27\frac{1}{2}''$). Press well.

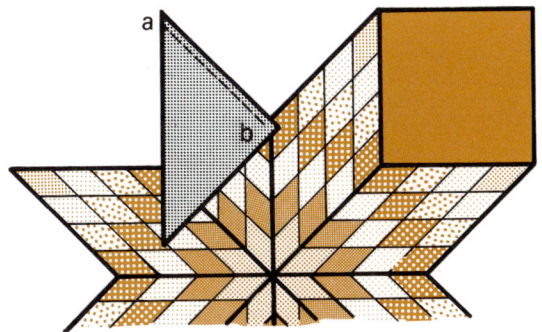

To make up the border

1 Make a square template 10 cm × 10 cm (or 4″ × 4″).

2 Choose a variety of different prints or plain fabrics, making sure you have some dark, some medium and medium/light, and some light. A possible way to arrange the borders would be like this: (ie. D = dark; L = light; M = medium; M/L = medium/light.)

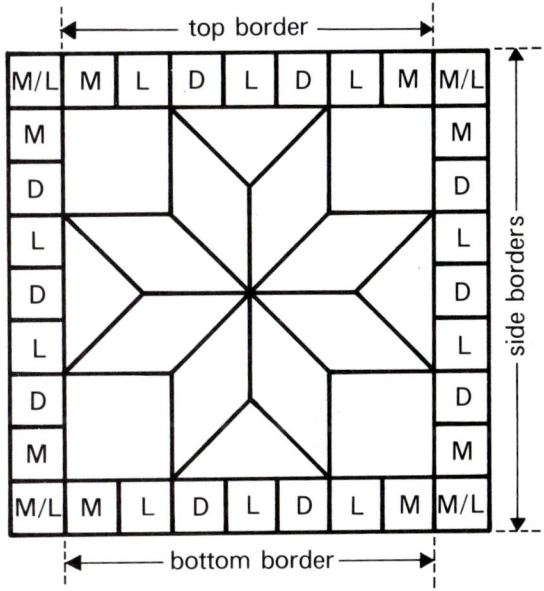

3 Placing the template on the wrong side of the fabric, mark out 32 squares – 10 dark, 10 light, 8 medium and 4 medium/light. Cut the patches leaving a seam allowance of 1 cm (or $\frac{3}{8}''$).

4 Pin the squares right sides together along the matched drawn lines and sew up into four strips. Tie and cut the threads, and press the seams one way.

5 Pin the top and bottom borders right sides together to the central square first and sew the seams. Press seams outwards. Then pin the side borders, matching the seams at the corners accurately, and sew. Tie and cut threads and press the cover well.

6 Make up the cushion cover according to the instructions on page 16. For a floor cushion, it is a good idea to use a hard wearing material, such as hessian, for the under side.

The Baby Blocks or Tumbling Blocks pattern in three cotton lawn prints gives this cot cover an interesting three-dimensional effect.

Detail of the pattern showing how the knotting gives the cover a quilted look.

COT COVER

This cot cover is made up of groups of three diamonds assembled to form a hexagon, giving the pattern a three-dimensional effect. To get this effect you must use one dark, one medium and one light coloured fabric. This pattern is called Baby Blocks or sometimes Tumbling Blocks, and there is another example of it on page 2.

The instructions are given for sewing by hand with paper patterns. Although we are not explaining quilting in this book – an art which needs a book to itself – we will show you the simple technique of knotting which gives a quilted look to this cot cover.

The overall size of the cover is 64 cm × 85 cm (or 25″ × 33½″). The border is 7 cm wide (or 2¾″) and the diamond has sides of 6 cm (or 2⅜″).

If you decide to change the measurements, work out the width of the border and size of the diamond carefully so that you can calculate the correct number of diamonds for your chosen size.

1 Buy or make a diamond template with sides 6 cm long (or 2⅜″). (See instructions on page 62.)

2 Now choose your fabrics. You will need one light, one medium and one dark in tone. Make sure you also have enough of the medium and light fabrics for the border. Wash and press them well. You will also need material for the backing (approx. 1 metre) and wadding if you intend to knot the cover.

3 Use the template to cut out 129 paper patterns on good quality thick paper, drawing closely round the template with a sharp pencil and cutting accurately along the lines.

4 You will need 40 patches of dark material, 40 patches of light material and 49 patches of medium material. Pin the paper patterns to the wrong side of the material and cut the patches with an allowance of 1 cm (or ⅜″) all the way round.

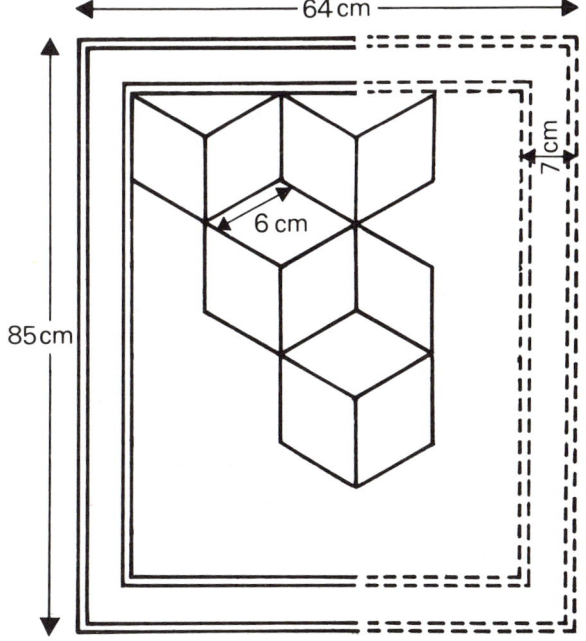

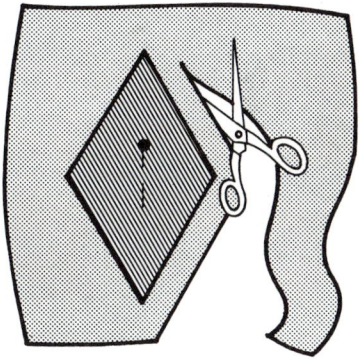

5 Thread a needle with tacking cotton but don't knot the thread. Tack the material to the paper by turning it over the edge of the paper. At the sharp corner, fold the material as shown, making sure the material fits snugly over the paper. Overlap the tacking stitches at the end.

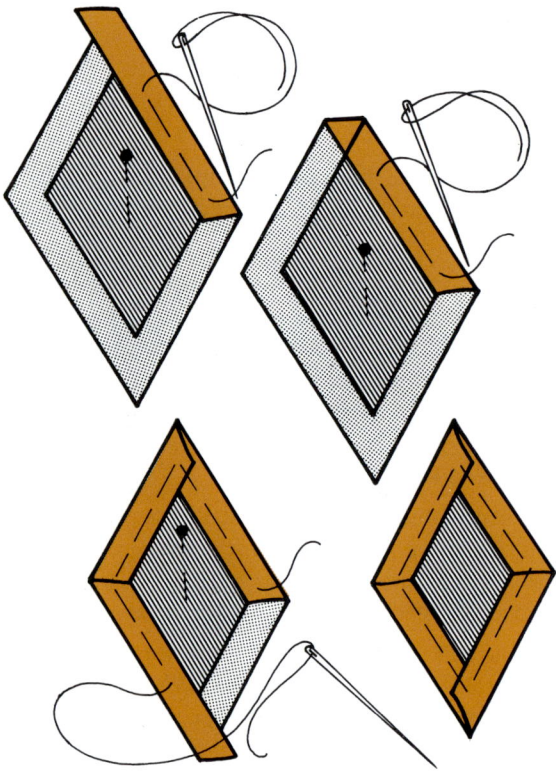

6 When all the patches are tacked, lay out the first strip of patches on newspaper in the three-dimensional pattern working across the width of the cover.

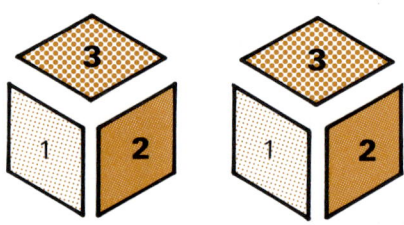

Thread a No. 8 or 9 needle with polyester cotton thread and make a good knot in the end of your thread. Take one light patch (1) and one dark patch (2) and place them right sides together. Put the needle in at the corner A underneath the material and make a double stitch at the corner for strength. Sew with small, firm, even oversewing stitches to join

the two edges from A to B, making a double stitch again at the corner B.

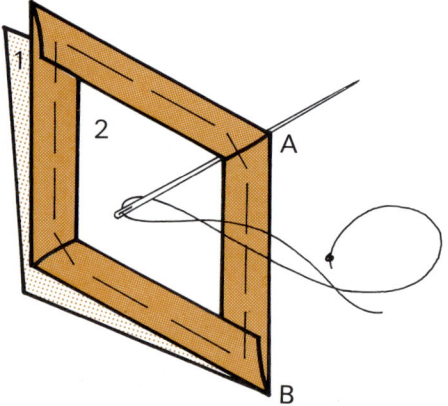

Open the two diamonds out, then take one medium patch (3) and place it right sides together with (2) and sew from C–D. Make a double stitch at D, then ease patch (3) right sides together with (1) and continue sewing to E. Make a double stitch.

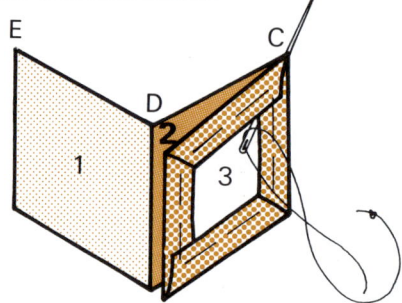

You may find it easier to work systematically, joining the first row into blocks of three, then the blocks into a strip. Then add the next row of medium patches, followed by the strip of alternating light and dark patches.

Continue until you have completed the patched area. Your edges will have extra half diamonds but these will disappear when you join the patchwork to the border.

To make the border

1 Start with the inside section of the border. Using the medium fabric, cut:
two strips 52 cm long (or 20½″) and 3.5 cm wide (or 1½″)
two strips 75 cm long (or 29¼″) and 3.5 cm wide (or 1½″).
Pin the first two strips right sides together with the patchwork along the top and bottom of the cover, leaving a seam allowance of 1 cm (or ⅜″).

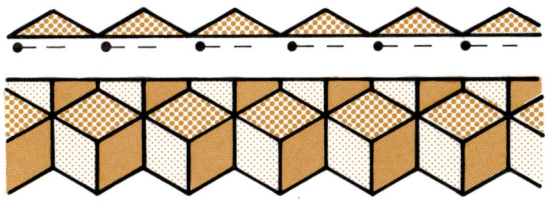

Sew the two borders to the patchwork. This is where your extra half diamonds along the edge disappear. Press the seams outwards. Pin the sew the two borders to the sides in the same way. Press well.

2 Next, using the light fabric, cut:
two strips 55.5 cm long (or 21¾″) and 6 cm wide (or 2½″)
two strips 84.5 cm long (or 33¼″) and 6 cm wide (or 2½″).
Pin and sew to the first section of the border in the same way as above. Press well.

3 Finally, using the medium fabric, cut:
two strips 64 cm long (or 25″) and 3.5 cm wide (or 1¼″)
two strips 86.5 cm long (or 34″) and 3.5 cm wide (or 1¾″).
Pin and sew to the middle section of the border in the same way as above. Press well.

To finish the cover

1 Cut out the backing material *1cm less all round* than the finished patchwork with border. If you do not want to knot the cot cover, ignore stages 2 and 3 and continue with No. 4.

2 Cut out the wadding the same size as the backing material. Pin the three layers together, patchwork top, wadding and backing, starting at the centre and working out towards the edges and corners, smoothing any wrinkles as you go. Tack the three layers together along the pin lines. Finally, tack all round the edges.

3 To knot the layers together, you will need a strong thread like crochet cotton. Do not use a synthetic thread as this will not retain the knot. The knots are made at each corner of your diamonds.
Starting at the centre of the quilt, take a stitch, pull the thread through leaving a tail of about 4 cm (or 1½″). Take a second stitch over the first and pull it tight.

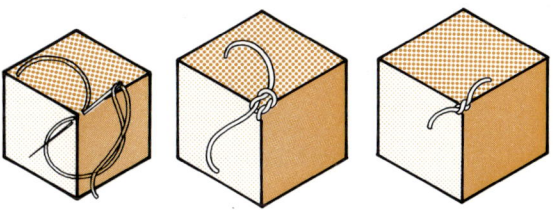

Tie the two ends together firmly in a reef knot. Snip the two ends to about 1.5 cm (or ½″). Tie a knot at every point of the diamonds, working out from the centre. Remove all the tacking threads and trim the edges of the backing and wadding.

4 If you have missed out stages 2 and 3, pin and tack the backing to the patchwork, starting at the centre and working outwards. Then turn the seam allowance on the edge of the outside border to the back. Turn under the raw edge, pin and slipstitch down all round the cover.

This picture shows how effective a collection of patchwork cushions can be if the colours are carefully chosen to blend well together.

These four cushions are all made up in the same Star of Bethlehem pattern but each one looks quite different because of the way the fabrics are used.

VARIATIONS ON A THEME

This collection of cushions shows how effective patchwork can be if the structure, tone and colour are all carefully thought out. It is perfectly possible to mix a number of different patterns together so long as the tones all blend well.

1 Have a look first at the four cushions on the opposite page whose technical structure is identical. It is the same pattern, the Star of Bethlehem, as the one used for the floor cushion illustrated on page 42. The clever use of colour in these four gives extraordinarily different effects. In three out of the four cushions six fabrics have been used and in one (top right) the lightest fabric is duplicated. The careful arrangement of tone, colour and contrast shows how the surface can be transformed. To make these cushions, decide on the size of your star and follow the instructions for the floor cushion on page 43. They all have solid rather than patched borders.

It is interesting to experiment with colour and tone. Successful patchwork depends entirely on getting proportion, tone and contrast sensitively balanced.

2 The first cushion on this page also shows how a structure – in this case a Log Cabin variation – can be transformed by the arrangement of tones. Instead of the usual dramatic light/dark contrasts of Log Cabin, these strip cushions are just as effective using, in the first one, two softly blending plain colours, pink and fawn, and in the second a mixture of blending prints.

To make the first cushion, choose two plain fabrics which blend well together. Cut a square and four triangles for the centre and long strips in your chosen width of each colour. Sew the four triangles on to the sides of the square (see instructions for this technique on page 40). Then sew two strips of the same colour to the top and bottom of the square and cut them to the width of the central square.

Next sew two strips of the *same* colour to the sides and cut to length. (Follow the same basic technique of sewing and cutting as described in the chapter on Log Cabin on page 27, but

instead of working clockwise round the centre, you sew the strips to the top and bottom first, then to the sides.)

Continue with the second colour sewing the strips as before.

Carry on building up your cover alternating the two colours round the central square until it is the right size. Make up the cover in the usual way (see page 16).

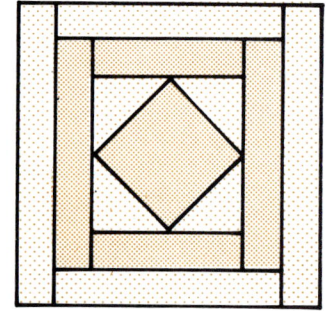

The second cushion on the previous page is made in exactly the same way except that the centre is one square, in this case a print with a floral medallion.

3 The strip can be used in other ways too. The cushion (top photograph this page) combines the eight-pointed star and the strips. The star forms the central medallion and it is framed by four broad strips, sewn on in the same way as described above.

On a larger scale, but still using the same idea of strips surrounding a central square, is the quilt (bottom photograph this page) which was made in England in 1825. It is a simple and attractive idea for a bed cover or tablecloth.

4 Finally, yet another use of the eight-pointed star in a pattern known as Jackson Star is shown in the photograph on the facing page. To make this pattern, you will need three or four fabrics in a mixture of prints and plain colours.

The templates are:
long diamond with sides 5 cm (or 2″)
square with sides 5 cm (or 2″)
right-angled triangle with equal sides 5 cm (or 2″).
From these you will need to cut:
32 diamonds, 20 squares, 8 triangles.
The patched area of the cushion is 30 cm × 30 cm (or 12″ × 12″) and it has a solid border 5 cm wide (or 2″).

However, before you decide on your fabrics, draw the pattern out and experiment with light and dark tones. These two diagrams show how the different use of tone changes the whole feel of the pattern. Make up the patched area using the method you have found suits you best, and make up the cover following the instructions on page 16.

These examples will give you a glimpse into the endless variety and challenge of patchwork, so beautifully summed up in this quotation from 'Aunt Jane of Kentucky' by Eliza Calvert Hall:
'How much piecin' a quilt is like livin' a life! Many a time I've set and listened to Parson Page preachin' about predestination and free will, and I've said to myself, "If I could jest git up there in the pulpit with one of my quilts, I could make life a heap plainer than parson's makin' it with his big words."
You see, to make a quilt you start out with jest so much caliker; you don't go to the store and pick it out and buy it, but the neighbors give you a piece here and there and you'll find you have a piece left over every time you've cut out a dress, and you jest take whatever happens to come. That's the predestination. But when it comes to cuttin' out the quilt,

why, you're free to choose your own pattern. You give the same kind of pieces to two persons and one'll make a "Nine-Patch" and the other one'll make a "Wild-goose-Chase" and so there'll be two quilts made of the same kind of pieces but jest as different as can be. That's the way of livin'. The Lord sends us the pieces; we can cut 'em out and put 'em together pretty much to suit ourselves. There's a heap more in the cuttin' out and the sewin' than there is in the caliker.'

53

Subtle purple, green and blue in a simple Centre Diamond pattern were chosen by the Amish housewife who made this quilt around 1900.

AMISH QUILT

This quilt was made around 1900 by a member of a group of people called the Amish. They are descendants of American settlers who in the 18th Century fled from religious persecution in Switzerland and Germany. Amish quilts have a distinct quality: their original designs and intense plain colours are the products of a community which has shunned the world and turned to a life close to the land, relying on the Bible to guide their behaviour.

The Amish were one of a number of Protestant sects who settled in America in the 1720s, mainly in Pennsylvania, Ohio and Indiana. They are named after Jacob Amman, a Mennonite bishop from Switzerland who founded his own sect in 1693 based upon the tenets of adult baptism, the refusal of military duty and the rejection of modern luxuries. In his day, these were the extravagances of the established churches in Europe. Today the strict Amish shun such products of progress as the car, telephone, electricity, television, tractors and even buttons on their clothing.

Their dress is plain and in their homes they have plain carpets and simple furniture, all of which are visible signs to the outside world that they are different – in the world but not 'of it'. However, colour is used in abundance. They often have brightly coloured flower gardens for which the women are responsible, as they are too for the subtle glowing colours of their quilts. They used large areas of cloth for their shapes to create astonishing abstract geometric compositions. Although they rejected patterned fabrics, they nevertheless quilted their bold areas of patchwork with an intricacy and flamboyance that must have satisfied some inner need. The intense, sometimes sombre colours, and bold designs make these quilts an important contribution to the art of patchwork. It is interesting to compare them with the abstract paintings of the twentieth century which they anticipated by several generations. In fact, you may find that a visit to an art gallery will give you inspiration for a bed cover – look for bold simple arrangements of shapes and interesting colour combinations.

The basic shapes used by the Amish women are the square, the rectangle and the triangle. The square set diagonally to form a diamond had a particular significance for them, representing the rock or corner-stone of their religion. The patchwork is very easy to make technically though whether or not it works visually depends on the use of colour. Over the page are some drawings of a range of Amish designs. Look for plain fabrics in good colours – cottons or fine wools in greys, browns, beiges, greens, blues, purples or reds, or curtain lining material which comes in a range of soft colours. Try not to use more than four colours in a cover – some of the most striking Amish quilts use only two or three. In fact, the effectiveness of much patchwork lies in the use of plain rather than printed fabrics.

Measure your bed and the overhang at the sides and bottom and make a scale drawing of your chosen design on paper. Choose your fabrics and cut out the shapes to the sizes you have worked out. The covers usually have a narrow border or binding round the edge. Follow the instructions for lining on p. 41.

It is interesting to compare the Amish quilts with the one shown on page 58. It was made in Wales around 1880 from fine plain wool in glowing red and beige and is intricately quilted with designs drawn from ancient Celtic art. There was no communication between the Welsh and the Amish – their only similarities were a frugal life and strict non-conformist religious beliefs. It is fascinating that the design and use of colour should be so similar.

Centre square   Centre square   Bars

Bars   Split bars   Centre diamond

Centre diamond   **Centre** diamond   Brick wall

1 Select eleven materials in bright colours in tones ranging from light to dark, preferably plain or else *very small* prints. The effect will be too busy if the designs are very prominent. Men's shirting material is good for this as the designs tend to be small and neat.

2 Mark out your pattern on graph paper numbering the colours in the squares as shown.

3 Make a square template with sides 4 cm (or 1½"). Wash and press your fabrics. On a firm surface, mark out on the wrong side of the material and cut leaving a seam allowance of 1 cm (or ⅜"). Cut a number of squares from all eleven fabrics, then as your patchwork grows, cut more when you need them.

4 To sew up, place the squares right sides together, pin and machine or sew by hand as for the Jacob's Ladder cushion (see page 36). Starting with square 1, make up the central patched square as marked. Then continue working in strips as follows: make two strips (a)–(b) and sew to the central square area. Then make two strips (x)–(y) and sew to the sides of the central square. Continue until your entire square is made up.

5 The border is made up of three strips of plain material, in this case orange, red and dark blue. Cut two strips from all three materials 5 cm wide (or 2") the length of the sides of the completed patchwork. Machine the three strips together. Press the seams open and join to the sides of the patchwork. Then cut two strips from each of the three colours 5 cm wide (or 2") the length of the top and bottom of the cover. Join the strips and sew to the patchwork in the same way. Press. Line and bind the edges following the instructions on page 41.

The quilt shown above and also in colour on the front cover, was a popular pattern among the settlers in Pennsylvania, including the Amish. It is called Trip Around the World but the Amish always called it Sunshine and Shadow. This quilt was made in Lancaster County, Pennsylvania between about 1880 and 1890 and consists of brightly coloured contrasting squares arranged in a diamond formation.

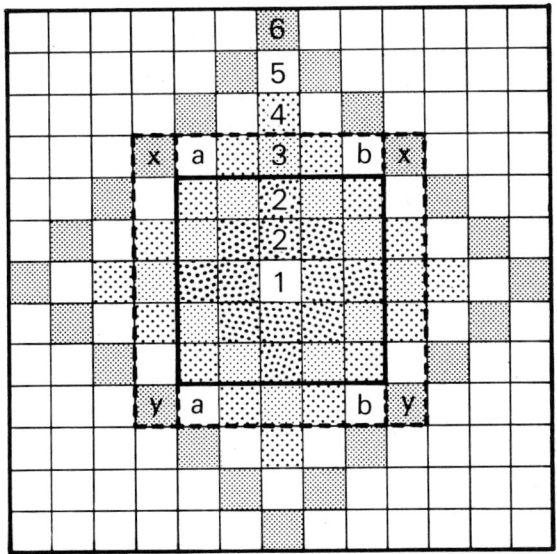

This quilt in glowing red and biege was made in Wales around 1880. It shows a remarkable similarity to the Amish quilts both in the pattern and the intricate quilting. (See p. 55.)

SELECTION OF AMERICAN BLOCK PATTERNS

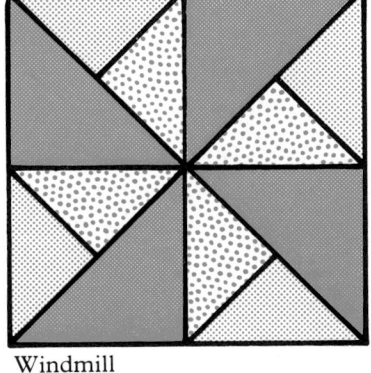

Windmill

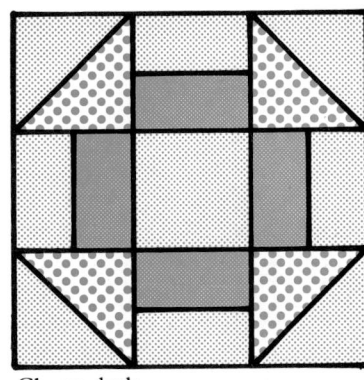

Churn dash

Indian hatchet

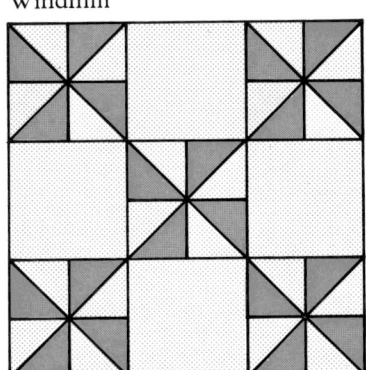

Pin wheels

Sister's choice

Beggar's blocks

Road to Oklahoma

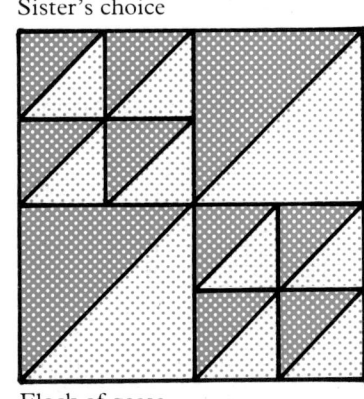

Flock of geese

Old Maid's puzzle

Kitty corner

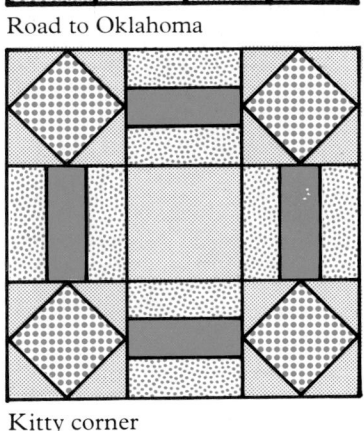

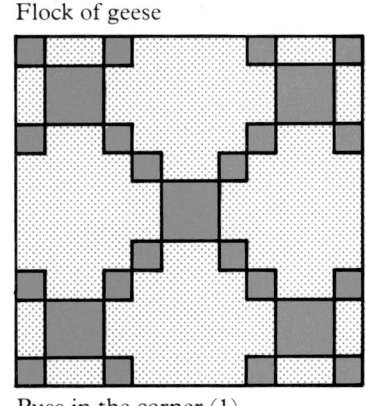

Puss in the corner (1)

59

Puss in the corner (2)

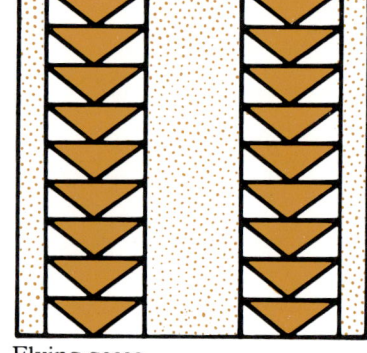

Flying geese

Goose tracks

Bear's paw

Further examples of Log Cabin arrangements

Weather vane

Indian trail

Barn raising

Windmill blades

Straight furrow

Light and dark (1)

Light and dark (2)

HOW TO MAKE YOUR OWN TEMPLATES

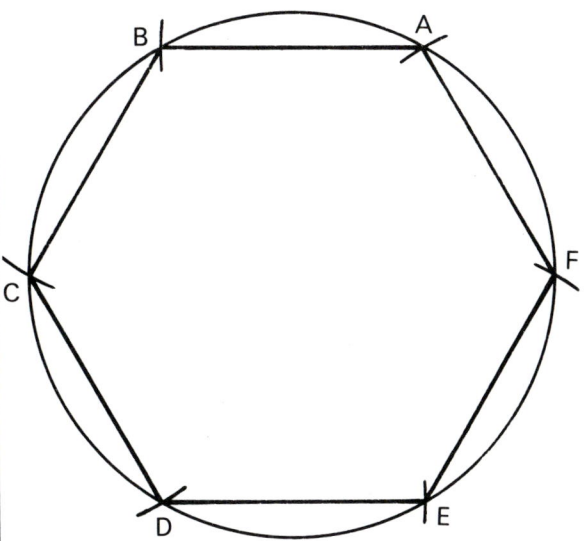

Home-made templates won't last as long as bought ones, but you can always be sure of having a wide range of shapes and sizes available at much less cost. If you are making a large article and have to cut a number of patches from the same template, it is a good idea to make several templates at the same time, so that when the first one loses its accuracy, you will always have another which you know is exactly the same. Some people bind the edges of the template with sellotape first to make it last longer.

For making your own templates, you will need the following equipment:

thick card, pair of compasses, protractor, lino-cutting knife, metal ruler, sharp pencil, board for cutting on.

Hexagon (six-sided shape)

1 Choose the size of the hexagon – that is, decide on the length of the sides.

2 Set the compasses to this measurement.

3 On thick card, draw a circle with the compasses set in this way.

4 *Keeping the compasses set the same*, put the point anywhere on the circumference of the circle – eg at point A – and draw an arc to cross at point B. Put the compasses point at B and draw another arc at C, and so on until six arcs have been made. The last one should cross the circle at A. (See top drawing.)

5 Join the points A–B–C–D–E–F with a ruler and a sharp pencil to make up the hexagon.

6 To cut out the hexagon, place the card on a board. Put a metal ruler along one edge (eg A–B), hold it down firmly and cut along the line with a lino-cutting knife. Repeat all around the hexagon until the shape is finished.

Square or rectangle

1 Choose the size of your square or rectangle – that is, decide on the length of the sides.

2 Draw a horizontal line and mark off your required length A–B.

3 Centre the protractor over A and mark an angle of 90°.

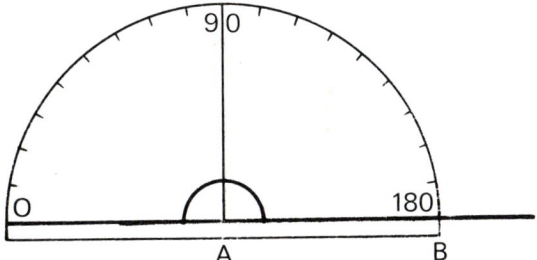

4 Mark off your required length A–C.

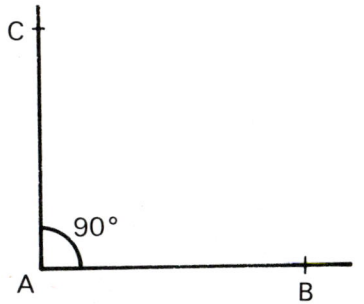

5 Centre the protractor over C and mark an angle of 90°. Draw the line C–D and mark off your required length.

6 Join points D–B to complete the square.

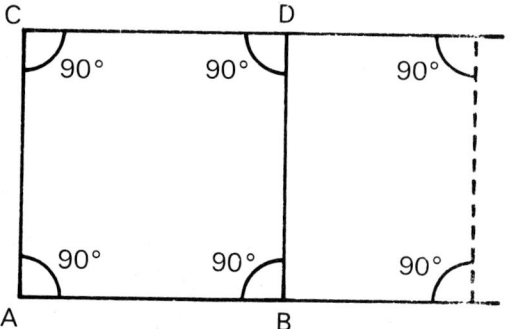

7 Cut out in the same way as for the hexagon.

Square

Another method of constructing a square is as follows:

1 Draw a horizontal line and mark three points x, y and z equidistant from each other.

2 Set the compasses to any length, but longer than x–z. Place the point at x and make an arc above point y. Place the point at z and make another arc to cross the first at A.

3 Join A to y.

4 Decide on the length of the sides of your square and set the compasses to this length.

5 Place the compasses point at y and make an arc to cross the line A–y at P, and another arc to cross the base line at Q.

6 *With the compasses still set the same*, place the point at P and make an arc above point Q. Set the point at Q and make an arc to cross the first at R.

7 With a ruler join points P–R and R–Q to form a square. Check with a protractor that your angles are all 90°.

8 Cut out in the same way as for the other templates.

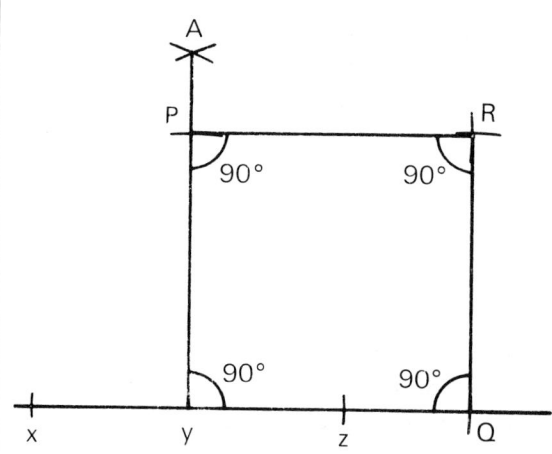

Diamond
(sometimes known as a lozenge)

This diamond is based on a hexagon and makes up a six-pointed star.

1 Decide on the length of the sides of the diamond and set the compasses to this measurement. On thick card, construct a hexagon to this size in the same way as above.

2 With a ruler and a sharp pencil, draw a line through points A–C and B–D.

3 The shaded areas make up the diamond shapes. Cut out the shapes in the same way as for the other templates.

Long diamond

This diamond is based on an octagon (eight-sided shape) and makes up an eight-pointed star.

1 Decide on the length of the sides of the diamond and set the compasses to this measurement.

2 On thick card, draw a circle with your set compasses.

3 Using a protractor, mark off from the central point O, angles of 45°.

4 Join points A–B–C–D–E–F–G–H to form an octagon.

5 *With the compasses still set at the same measurement*, place the point at A and make an arc outside the circle between points A and B.

6 Place the point of the compasses at B and make another arc to cross the first one at Z.

7 Join points A–Z and B–Z to make a diamond.

8 Cut out as for the other templates.

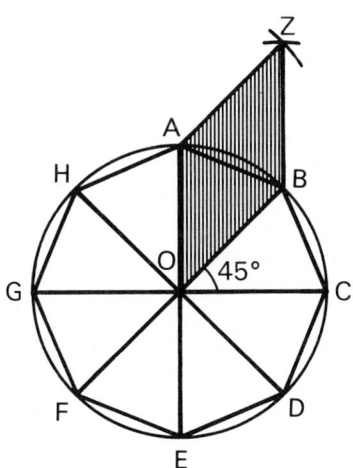

Triangle

There are two kinds of triangles most commonly used in patchwork. The first is made by dividing a square diagonally to give you a right-angled triangle.

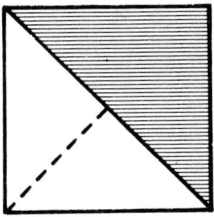

The second is made by dividing a diamond in half.

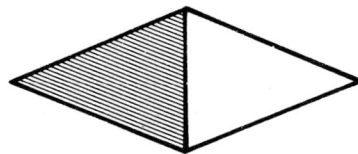

Window templates

Window templates made of clear plastic with a shaded area round the edge are available from craft shops. Some people find them useful for selecting certain parts of a pattern – for example, getting a floral motif centred on a patch. The shaded area of the template is the seam allowance. The template is placed on the material and the patches marked and cut out. It is primarily of use if you are making patchwork with paper patterns.

Another form of window template is extremely useful as it enables you to draw not only the sewing line but also the cutting line on the material. If you prefer, you can make all your templates in this way.

Draw out your shape on card in the ways described above, then leaving 1 cm (or ⅜″) for the seam allowance, draw another shape outside the first one. Cut out along both the inside and outside lines.

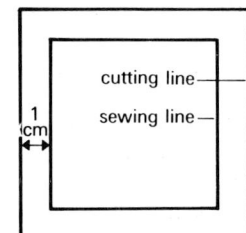

Place your template on the material and draw round the inside and outside lines. The inside line is the sewing line and gives you the size of your finished patch and the outside line is the cutting line.

BOOKLIST AND ADDRESSES

BANNISTER, B. and FORD, E. *United States patchwork pattern book* Dover Publishers, 1976.

BISHOP, R. *New discoveries in American quilts* E. P. Dutton, 1977.

BISHOP, R. and SAFANDA, E. *A gallery of Amish quilts* E. P. Dutton, 1977.

BOGEN, C. *Beginner's book of patchwork, appliqué and quilting* Nelson, 1976.

COLBY, A. *Patchwork quilts* Batsford, n.i. 1975.

FITZRANDOLPH, M. and FLETCHER, F. M. *Quilting: traditional methods and design* Dryad Press, 1968.

GOLDEN HANDS SPECIAL *Patchwork and appliqué* Marshall Cavendish, 1976. op.

GONIN, E. and NEWTON, J. *Quilt making* Octopus Books, 1974. op.

ICKIS, M. *The standard book of quilt making and collecting* Dover Publications, 1949.

IVES, S. *Patterns for patchwork quilts and cushions* Batsford, 1977.

McKIM, R. S. *One hundred and one patchwork patterns* Dover Publications, 1963.

PARR, S. ed. *Patchwork and appliqué* Marshall Cavendish, 1977.

Places to visit

Victoria and Albert Museum, London
American Museum in Britain, Claverton Manor, Bath
Welsh Folk Museum, St. Fagan's, Cardiff
Gawthorpe Hall, Padiham, Nr. Burnley, Lancs. (a small selection of textiles is on view during National Trust opening times but serious students should contact the Lecturer Curator for permission to view the more extensive collection)
The Bowes Museum, Barnard Castle, Co. Durham (collection of quilts and coverlets can be seen by appointment)

Back cover: Patchwork cushions in blending colours give a lively touch in any room.

Suppliers of material

Here are some firms which supply material suitable for patchwork by mail order. Write to these addresses, enclosing a stamped addressed envelope, for catalogues and order forms:

Laura Ashley
Box No 1,
Mail Order Department,
Carno,
Powys,
Wales

J. W. Coates & Co. Ltd.,
Croft Mill,
Lowther Lane,
Foulridge,
Colne,
Lancashire BB8 7NG

M. Lord & Sons,
Acre Mill,
Farholme Lane,
Stacksteads,
Bacup,
Lancashire

Acknowledgements

We are grateful to the following for permission to reproduce photographs of their work:

JOEN ZINNI Block patterns page 6, Jacob's Ladder cushion page 34

ROSAMOND RICHARDSON Pincushions page 10, cot cover page 13, Nine-Patch cushions page 14, shopping bags page 18, borders page 22, Log Cabin bag page 29, skirt page 33, block cushions page 37, floor cushion page 42

LUCY GOFFIN Quilt page 13, cushion page 21

GILL HOWELL (for Caroline Watt Designs) Log Cabin cushion page 26

DAWN PAVITT Waistcoat page 30, cushions page 50 and back cover

DEIRDRE AMSDEN Cot cover page 46

SARAH FROST made up the items illustrated on pages 10 and 22

Acknowledgement is due to the following for permission to reproduce quilts from their collections:

JOEN ZINNI Front cover and page 57, page 39
JANE KASMIN, RON SIMPSON, PAUL TAYLOR Page 2, page 21, page 38, page 39, page 52, page 58
MRS. BAGOT AND VICTORIA AND ALBERT MUSEUM Page 4
JOY WILCOX Page 54